"WHY ME?
WHY ANYONE? WHY?"

Nancy Kerrigan was in Detroit for the National Figure Skating Championship when the vicious beating left her in intense pain and stunned bewilderment. But the love and support of her family that had sustained her through the years and enabled her to pursue her goals now provided the courage and morale she needed to make a remarkable recovery.

Nancy's father was a Massachusetts welder who took second jobs and remortgaged the family home so she could pursue her dreams on the ice. The sacrifices he and her family made were well worth it. Through determination, hard work, and perseverance, Nancy rocketed through the ranks of America's figure skaters, in five years going from being ranked twelfth to being ranked second in the nation when she took the Olympic bronze in 1992.

This is Nancy's story—through victories, heartaches, and, ultimately, her renewed determination to compete and win.

Also by Randi Reisfeld:

MELROSE PLACE: Meet the Stars of the Hottest TV
  Show
THE STARS OF BEVERLY HILLS 90210: Their Lives
  and Loves
LOVIN' LUKE: The Luke Perry Story
MARKY MARK AND THE FUNKY BUNCH
THE OFFICIAL BAYWATCH FACT FILE
SO YOU WANT TO BE A STAR! A Teenager's Guide
  to Breaking into Show Business

THE BAR/BAT MITZVAH SURVIVAL GUIDE
WHEN NO MEANS NO: A Guide to Sexual Harassment (coauthor)

THE
KERRIGAN
COURAGE

Nancy's Story

Randi Reisfeld

BALLANTINE BOOKS • NEW YORK

ISBN 0-345-39084-9

Manufactured in the United States of America

First Edition: February 1994

10 9 8 7 6 5 4 3 2 1

Contents

Acknowledgments

The author gratefully acknowledges . . .

For making this book happen—and so quickly! . . .
Matthew Shear, Jeff Doctoroff, Evan Gourvitz, Nora
Reichard, and the staff at Ballantine Books; and
Stacey Woolf of Bob Woolf Associates

*For being the best, fastest, most detailed and ob-
sessive researcher in the world, and a great friend,
too* . . .
Janet Macoska

For sharing their memories of Nancy Kerrigan . . .
Jeff Gutridge, Thomas Ryan, William Orman, Bill

Mucica, Lydia Breen, Pat Norelli, Howard Dimmick, Jane Gagnon, Sally Sabo, Louise Case, Pat Kilty, and Connie at the Stoneham Public Library

For more helpful information . . .
Kevin Lowery, Jonathan Nettelfield, John Austin, and Linda Ivey Miller

For the flowers, the food, the feedback—for putting up with me and doing everything else while I was doing this . . .
Marvin, Scott, Stefanie, and my extended family of relatives and friends

For not standing outside my office and barking . . .
Peabo

Introduction

The image of an elegant, swanlike ballerina gliding effortlessly across the ice is what often comes to mind when we think about figure skating. But the events of the past month have left us with another image of the sport, one not nearly as graceful or beautiful. When a baton-wielding thug smashed Olympic hopeful Nancy Kerrigan across the knee, the "ice princess sport" took on a new face: one twisted with shock, pain, and fear. Though she never expected it or asked for it, Nancy Kerrigan was thrust into the limelight as the public face of the sport. The whole world witnessed as she bore the unbearable pain and shock of her assault; the whole world watched and waited to see if her physical and emotional wounds would heal in time for her to represent her country at the Olympic Games. It was a test of time, and, even more, a test of courage.

What the world *doesn't* know and hasn't seen, however, is that this is hardly the first time this remarkable young woman has been tested. Courage isn't something she's developed recently, after the brutal attack that threatened the career she's pursued for her entire life. Courage is something she's had to rely on repeatedly over the years.

Since she started skating, Nancy Kerrigan, the small-town girl with the great big talent, has had to find the courage . . .

. . . not to quit when the pain was so bad, she could barely walk

. . . not to quit when no matter how hard she tried, she just could not perfect a move

. . . not to quit when the expenses for her skating outweighed her dad's yearly salary

. . . not to quit when she had to choose between having a social life and skating

. . . not to quit in the face of public humiliation on national television

. . . not to quit when her own inner demons said, "You can't, you're no good, you'll fail

. . . and certainly not to quit just because some unscrupulous individuals thought she should.

The Nancy Kerrigan story is about where that courage comes from. It's about her family, her roots, her hometown. It's about finding the courage of confidence, about learning to believe in yourself. It's about something else, too. In the words of a former professional ice skater, "Skating competition is not so much a contest to win medals. It is more a test of one's courage, a measure of one's character. Even if disaster strikes—a not infrequent occurrence when poised on blades a fraction of an inch wide—one must never waver." This Nancy knows to be true, in the deepest sense. This is who she is.

CHAPTER ONE

Go Figure: "Ice Skating Was Something to Do, Just for Fun"

Those who know Nancy Kerrigan understand where she's from and where she's coming from: in spirit, pride, stick-to-itiveness, an uncanny ability to overcome obstacles, and what we still call all-American values. In all of these qualities, she is an absolute reflection of her family and of her hometown. She had many profiles in courage to emulate.

You wouldn't have said there was anything unusual about the Kerrigans. There was no clue, early on, that this family was destined for anything beyond their own modest dreams: good educations for this children, a small home of their own, and enough money to take an annual family vacation skiing in the nearby hills of New Hampshire. In that way, they were no different than most folks in their hometowns. Daniel Kerrigan and his family were natives of Woburn, Massachusetts, a small industrial city where people worked hard and enjoyed the simple pleasures of Sunday sports and home-cooked family dinners. Brenda Schultz lived in neighboring Stoneham, a fiercely independent small town with no shopping malls or movie theaters, but a huge library and several well-appointed churches. Both Woburn and Stoneham are places where neighbors naturally pitch in to help one another—and everyone knows everyone else's business. Both towns are minutes from cosmopolitan Boston, but neither has the look or feel of a suburb. The townspeople don't feed off of "Beantown" for their livelihoods, culture, or identities. If you're from Woburn or Stoneham, you most likely are educated there, work there, and stay there. Roots run deep in this area, and that's just the way people like it. It is a source of pride.

When Brenda and Dan married and started their family, they lived in East Woburn, Their sons, Mark and Michael, were born there, and so, in October 1969, was their only daughter, Nancy Ann. Dan, an affable, easygoing man, supported the family by working as a welder at the General Foods–

Atlantic Gelatin plant just a few miles from home. Gregarious Brenda capably cared for the kids—cooking, carpooling, and coffee-clatching with other young mothers in the area. It was the life she expected and enjoyed.

To any observer, they looked like an average American family very typical of their time and place. But a tragic and bizarre twist of fate would prove just how above-average the Kerrigans really were. When they were blindsided by adversity, they reacted with extraordinary pluck, spirit, and courage. Yet they never considered themselves to be anything more than simple, average working people who coped. "You do what you have to, you get by," might be their credo.

Certainly, when Brenda Kerrigan looked lovingly into the shining blue eyes of her one-year-old daughter, Nancy, she couldn't possibly have known it would be the last time she'd ever see that face—or anything else—clearly. She couldn't have known that from that moment forward, memories and the vision in her mind's eye would have to suffice.

The tragedy struck silently as Brenda was driving around Stoneham one day with all three kids in the car. Suddenly, without warning, her vision blurred. She went to the local eye doctor, then to a series of specialists. Days passed, then weeks and months: it never cleared up. The eventual medical diagnosis was as bewildering as it was bizarre—her retinas had been damaged by multiple neuritis, a rare virus that had attacked the nerves in her eyes. "I've never had any pain, it was just a rare virus, like you'd get a common cold," she would explain years later. Although the virus itself might have been treatable at some point, complications led to a permanent deterioration of her vision. She lost all sight in her left eye and can see just a "teeny amount" out of the inside corner of her right eye.

The Kerrigans barely paused to feel sorry for themselves but took immediate, practical action; they did what they had to. Hiring household help was never within their emotional or financial realm. Instead, they turned to their family. That's what you do when the chips are down. A move to Stoneham seemed to be the obvious choice—Brenda's parents, George and Mary, and her brother and sister-in-law still lived there, so the Kerrigans would get plenty of help. They bought a one-hundred-year-old, two-story wood frame house on a narrow, hilly, winding street. Just a few blocks off Stoneham's Main Street, their new residence was two doors away from the elder Schultz's terraced white home.

Situated just where the street curves, the house is at the bottom of a downward-sloping, four-car-long driveway, far enough from the street so the Kerrigan kids could play in the front or backyard safely. Brenda quickly became familiar with her surroundings: she learned to navigate around the new house so well that she felt comfortable caring for her family there. As long as the kids were close to her, she could see them; it was only at a distance that she couldn't tell what was happening. In fact, with the help of their extended family, the Kerrigans' lives took on a real semblance of routine and normalcy. Much of the laundry, shopping, and some of the cooking fell to Dan; the carpooling was split between Brenda's mom, Mary, and other family members and neighbors. Still, no one complained or felt there was anything unusual about the arrangement. Mary Schultz cooked Sunday breakfast for everyone, every week. It was her pleasure.

More than anything, the Kerrigans were determined that their kids' lives be affected as little as possible by Brenda's disability. And as time went on, it was something they all took for granted, and as kids to, they adjusted. Mark, who is the only one of the brood who remembers a time when Brenda could see, recalled, "If you left a note for Mom, you wrote it in big letters." Because of the possibility that Brenda might trip on some misplaced object, the kids kept the house free of clutter. "But you could get away with a few things too, like a dirty face or dirty hands at the dinner table," Mark has said, "but if you wore a baseball cap at dinner, you'd hear, 'Take that hat off!' "

Perhaps it was their mom's disability that brought the Kerrigan kids closer than most siblings. Although they had the usual share of sibling rivalries and bickering, they also stuck close to one another. "My kids always played a lot of games together," Brenda recalled. One of those games was ice hockey.

Because Stoneham happens to be home to a huge indoor ice arena, hockey is one of the most popular pursuits for the town's children. There are several hockey leagues in town, and area schools have teams, too. Most kids learn to skate by first grade.

Like many other boys in town, both Mark and Michael Kerrigan were quick with a hockey stick and smooth skaters. *Unlike* most little girls at the time, however, so was Nancy Kerrigan. Even as a preschooler, Nancy was as athletic, quick, and competitive as her older brothers. Off the ice, they let her play with them and taught her the ropes. Nancy's favorite position was goalie—she even wore a mask! In no time at all, she developed a real talent and affinity for the sport. "I would skate around the house like a hockey player," Nancy remembered. She was anxious to demonstrate her skills on the ice just like her big brothers, but she hit one little snag. In fact, though Nancy maintains that "hockey is *not* how I started skating," it may very well have been the result of old-fashioned sexism that Nancy Kerrigan would one day become the world's most beloved figure skater. For there were no hockey lessons for girls, nor any girls' hockey "league of their own" for her to join. "In those days, they didn't let girls play hockey," Nancy has explained.

So the active, athletic, competitive little girl turned to the next best thing—an activity the ice arena *did* offer for girls—figure skating. In the very beginning, then, Nancy didn't have a burning desire to figure skate; she'd probably never even heard of Peggy Fleming or Dorothy Hamill. "It was something to do just for fun," she has related.

At six years old, Nancy was enrolled in the Learn to Figure Skate class at the Stoneham Ice Arena, less than a half mile from her house. Driven by her grandma, her dad, or a neighbor, she went once-a-week for a one-hour group lesson. Brenda Kerrigan came along too and sat in the stands with the other parents. In those days, "I could see a little of what was going on," she's said. She could see that Nancy liked the Learn to Figure Skate class, but then again, Nancy liked a lot of sports. And skating lessons weren't the only lessons she took. "I tried everything," Nancy has noted, "ballet lessons, swimming lessons, skiing lessons."

By the time Nancy entered first grade at nearby Emerson Elementary School, the Kerrigans had accomplished what they'd hoped: they were leading lives as close to normal as they could. All three kids had their after-school activities; each did homework and chores. Mostly, they enjoyed being together as a family. "We would go snowmobiling or skiing in New Hampshire," Brenda said, explaining that she, too, could ski, as long as she followed closely behind a guide who called out instructions such as "move right" or "move left." Describing their lives back then, Brenda added, "We're the type of family that even spends New Year's Eve together. We'd go to the same parties as the kids."

The Kerrigan's daily routine would be a not-so-extraordinary accomplishment for most families, but just by living active, full, and normal lives, Brenda and Dan Kerrigan set an example that Nancy has never forgotten. In the face of adversity, you don't fold or create narrower limits for your life. Instead, you summon up all your strength and courage, and carry on as best you can, to the fullest extent you can. You simply find a way to cope.

The hard-won normalcy of their lives, of course, was about to be challenged once again: this time, not be an affliction, but by their daughter's ability. As Nancy progressed through her earliest skating lessons, she began to demonstrate a real talent on ice. While most of her classmates were still trying to get up on the ice without promptly falling down again, or were learning to glide across the rink by pushing off a stanchion, Nancy began to pull away from the pack, not only standing and gliding gracefully but sketching spins.

Usually, it takes five to seven years for young skaters to move up the ladder of proficiency by earning their six Basic Badges: Nancy zipped through her early training in half that time. By the age of eight, she'd mastered everything from getting up from a kneeling position, to combination moves including forward and backward crossovers, the two-foot spin, continuous forward two-foot sways, and other complicated moves. Also, she wasn't afraid of falling down. If she fell, she shrugged it off, got up, and tried again.

Her talent didn't go unnoticed. With typical modesty, Dan Kerrigan related, "Someone said Nancy had real talent, back when she was very young. So we took it one step at a time."

The steps that you take when figure skating talent is apparent are these: first, join a Figure Skating Club, and then get a private coach. There are many clubs, but only some are sanctioned by the official U.S. Figure Skating Association (USFSA). Skaters who eventually hope to compete professionally need to be affiliated with the USFSA. Since the Kerrigans couldn't afford a private coach right away, *their* next step was semiprivate classes for Nancy, plus membership in the Stoneham Figure Skating Club—an officially sanctioned USFSA group.

But that quickly proved to be just a stopgap measure. In order to go further, Nancy would need private professional coaching. At eight years old, she began private lessons with such local coaches as Ducky Antonucci, Jackie Little, and Theresa Martin. Under their tutelage, she went far beyond the basics. The goal was to get her ready to pass the figures and freestyle testing program prescribed by the USFSA and to enter competitions. Naturally, there are different levels of competition: a talented young skater on his or her way to becoming a pro looks to advance through such rankings as Preliminary, Juvenile, Intermediate, Novice, Junior, and Senior. At each of those levels, there are many opportunities to compete locally, regionally, and then on a multistate level.

After a year of private lessons, Nancy was ready to enter her first competition. Along with other young skaters, ten-year-old Nancy Kerrigan proudly represented the Stoneham Figure Skating Club at the Boston Open. She came home with a second-place finish. Although her parents couldn't have been prouder, Nancy downplayed her triumph. "A lot of the skaters started competitions much younger, but my coach wouldn't let us. He wouldn't let us do it until we had an Axel."

What Nancy's referring to is a complicated maneuver—jumping in the air on one skate from a forward position, turning one and a half revolutions and landing on the opposite skate going backward. She was on her way to mastering this by the age of ten.

Nancy was clearly talented and, perhaps more importantly, was developing a true love for the sport, but neither she nor any of the other Kerrigans had begun to dream about her competing on a national level, let alone in the Olympics. Yet as she competed more often, even on local levels, they proudly delivered photos of Nancy and her team to the local newspaper. Still, not even Nancy was thinking much beyond the next step. Her sole motivation to continue, she has always maintained, is simple: "I just wanted to keep doing better."

That motivation, seemingly modest, would take the entire Kerrigan clan further than they or anyone ever could have predicted.

CHAPTER TWO

A Balancing Act: Skating & School

"How High I Aim, How Much I see,
How Far I Reach, Depends on Me"

That's a direct quote from *Wild Life*, the 1987 Stoneham High School Yearbook. The quote, of course, belongs to Nancy Kerrigan. Clearly, by her high school years, Nancy's focus had shifted, from simply wanting to do better in whatever the next competition was to aiming much, much higher. In fact, that shift took place just as she was entering her teen years *and* entering junior high school as well. Her stand-out record in local competitions was one reason; the urging of her coaches was another. Combined with Nancy's ever-increasing love for the ice rink and her growing dedication to the sport, these factors provided enough motivation for Nancy and parents to seriously consider taking it one step further.

During her grade-school years, Nancy had first competed on the Preliminary level, then advanced to the Juvenile level. In order to move up to the Intermediates, she would need to pass a series of tests in both figure and freestyle skating. Once she passed, she could represent her skating club in not only local but regional (in her case, New England) and what is called sectional (the Eastern part of the United States) competitions. This is how young skating hopefuls climb the ladder that eventually leads to the Olympics. It's the only way: there are no shortcuts. Often, the move from Juvenile to Intermediate is the point at which skaters who show extraordinary talent start to think about leaving home to train in professional facilities with other young prodigies under Olympic-level coaches. That was simply not an option for Nancy at this point— not only did the Kerrigans not have the means to finance such a training, they didn't have it in their hearts to send Nancy to live somewhere else. They elected to help her get to the next level by doing whatever they had to, right there in Stoneham.

It wasn't going to be easy. Nancy would train at the Stoneham arena for five hours a day—

whenever she could get "ice time" The arena was a very popular facility, used by many ice skating and hockey clubs, so ice time was not always easy to get. Nor was it cheap. Plus, Nancy had to design a practice schedule around school. It was the beginning of many years of sacrifice and lost sleep, as the Kerrigans adapted to one of the most punishing schedules ever endured by a teenage ice skater and her family.

Brenda Kerrigan described the kind of hours the family would keep: "Nancy and I would get up at four-thirty every morning; then I'd wake Dan up. I'd make Nancy's breakfast—what's the big deal about a glass of juice and a bowl of cereal? Dan would drive her over to the rink at six A.M., get on the Zamboni (an ice-resurfacing machine) to make the first ice, take a nap while she practiced, drive her to school, and then go to work himself."

After school, Nancy would go back to the rink and practice for two more hours. "Then I'd come home, eat dinner, do my homework, and go to sleep at seven," Nancy has recounted. The Kerrigans, daughter and parents, would continue this demanding routine for eight long years.

"We took it one step at a time," Dan Kerrigan maintains with plain-speaking modesty. "Every year, she had a little goal. And every year, she went a little further. But there was never any question,

never any pressure on Nancy. We always told her
that if she wanted to quick, she could quit."

Although Nancy *never* seriously considered quitting, there were times when she'd return home from
her afternoon practices whipped—and frustrated. It
was at those times that Brenda Kerrigan stepped
in—with a gentle encouraging nudge, and with her
own courage. For as the years progressed and
Brenda's eyesight steadily weakened, her brave
spirit only strengthened. Instead of saying, "I can't
do this," or "I quit" she took on yet more activities,
adding aerobics classes and even learning to water
ski. Facing down the fear of getting hurt is something Nancy learned from her mother. Years later,
Nancy would say, "My mom has always been my
biggest fan." Years earlier, Nancy was her mom's
biggest fan.

In September 1981, Nancy entered Stoneham
Junior High School. With wispy, wavy, shoulder-
length hair parted down the middle and brushed behind her ears, Nancy looked no different from the
other three hundred or so preteens in grades seven
and eight. But looks can be deceiving: even though
she attended classes with her peers and was generally well-liked, she was never quite "one of them."
For most adolescents, junior high school is the time
when girls discover boys—and soon after, vice

versa—the time when friendships start to become vital. Being "in with the crowd" (or at least, not an outsider) seems to be the most important thing in the world. Nancy Ann Kerrigan wasn't really in with any crowd, not at school anyway.

For one thing, she came to school late and left early, every single day. William Orman, principal of Stoneham Junior High School (now known as Stoneham Middle School) was vivid memories of his now-famous charge. "I clearly remember Nancy's grandmother driving her mother here to ask if they could make arrangements for Nancy to come in late, so she could get more skating time in. She'd have to miss most of first period, which was home economics." Making exceptions to the school rule wasn't something the administration did often, or easily. "After all," as Mr. Orman noted, "a lot of kids in this town skate," but it was clear that the Kerrigans cared as much about Nancy's education as they did about her skating. They assured the principal that she would make up any work she missed. It was a vow Nancy would keep—for the rest of her academic life.

Sally Sabo served as Nancy's guidance counselor for junior high, and she, too, was involved in structuring a schedule that met Nancy's basic academic needs while freeing up her skating time. "Nancy was very quiet, shy, demure—and polite," Ms.

Sabo says. "She was the kind of kid who'd say 'thank you very much' all the time. She never demanded your time or attention in any way—she was very self-sufficient, came in and did her work."

Nancy never talked about her skating at school. Perhaps she was afraid she'd be seen as a braggart; more likely, keeping her accomplishments to herself is just her nature. She probably didn't think there was anything to brag about. Ms. Sabo doesn't see anything terribly unusual about the young girl she knew. "Nancy was typical of a lot of kids at this school who compete in sports. She's really very typical of a lot of kids who come through this school system and live in this town; dignified, goal-oriented, with a strong work ethic. She's not flashy—she just does it. Stoneham is not a ritzy suburb. It's filled with a lot of hardworking people who have very high goals for their children."

Jane Gagnon was Nancy's home economics teacher, both in seventh and eighth grades. She clearly remembers a "petite, sweet, and shy Nancy Ann who'd quietly enter the room midway through the class, never causing a stir. She just came in and did her work. The other kids in the class accepted the arrangement; no one made a big deal over it." The subject matter consisted of units of baby-sitting, simple sewing, and cooking. If Nancy missed a class, she'd use a study period or stay after school to make up all tests and written work. A recipe, however, she might take home to do. "She was an average student who worked really hard to maintain her grades," Mrs. Gagnon says. "I'm sure it was a struggle with all the time she put in skating, but what I remember most clearly about Nancy was her smile. Her great, big smile." Nancy gave her a particularly sweet one the day her teacher said, "Someday, I'll see you at the Olympics."

Not everyone believed it, of course. There's a tale told so often these days in Stoneham, it's taken on an almost legendary air. "We used to have this vice-principal, up at the high school," Ms. Sabo chuckled. "He was a kind of curmudgeonly type— very good with the kids, but kind of gruff, you know. At one point, it was his job to arrange a customized schedule for Nancy around her skating time. The Kerrigans also asked him to waive the 'eight unexcused absences and you fail the course' rule, knowing full well Nancy would be absent many more times than that. He wasn't exactly happy to have to do it, and one day he burst out with, 'My God, Nancy, you'd think you were going to the Olympics or something!' He was joking . . . but not entirely!"

Back on the ice rink, Nancy was progressing nicely. She'd made it to the Intermediate level by eighth grade and was getting more involved in competitions. In spite of her ever-increasing proficiency on ice, those events did not always go well for Nancy. Although she was steadily advancing on the whole, it was never a straight route to the top. She often came up short, returning home with neither medal nor commendation, only a sore backside from a difficult fall. The losses only shored up her resolve to do better, however: this attitude became stronger and stronger each year. In some ways, the losses are what propelled Nancy to keep going: "I just know I can do better," she'd always say—and look for the chance to prove it.

Even as early as junior high school, the competitions she was involved in, would often take her away from class—sometimes for a day, sometimes for as long as a week. If being completely focused on skating and coming in late to class weren't enough to put a crimp in her social life, certainly the lengthy and every more frequent absences were. "I don't remember Nancy having a lot of friends in junior high—her brother Michael was the outgoing one," is Ms. Sabo's recollection. While she wasn't surrounding herself with school friends, Nancy seemed to be getting even closer to her family. Just at the time most kids are taking their first tentative steps away from their families, Nancy seemed to be pulling in even tighter. "She was very close with them; they played a major role in her life back then," Ms. Gagnon says. "But they didn't push her. I remember Nancy once telling me that her parents pledged to support her—as long as it was what she wanted to do."

Nancy started her freshman year at Stoneham High School in the fall of 1983, and once again, the first order of business was securing a schedule that would allow her to skate in the wee hours of the morning, come late to school, and leave early to return to the rink. That job fell to the principal, Thomas Ryan. "It actually worked out fine," he said. "We were able to work out a schedule where she'd leave after the first three or four periods to get her ice time in—and make sure she got all her majors in as well. Nancy shouldered a regular academic course load that would prepare you for college, but just majors like English, history, math, and science, nothing more. She was very firm that skating was going to be her life. I used to try to convince her to take an extra course in case she changed her mind. 'What if you want to pursue something else?' I'd say, but she would hear none of it. She said very clearly that skating was her life and that's what she was going to do—she'd do anything toward that end. Her goal at that point wasn't necessarily even the Olympics—she just wanted to keep skating and keep getting better at it, and moving up. At school, she wanted to take [the courses that were] required, and would accomplish her high school program. She was going to be a skater and that was that."

Mr. Ryan admits that he was impressed with Nancy's determination. "I thought it was kind of amazing for someone to be so sure of herself at that time in her life—she was so small and quiet, not someone who took your breath away." He was also a little doubtful. "After all, she was good. She was at the level where she had a private coach and was competing on a national circuit—but she was no phenom. She was no Michelle Kwan. A lot of kids think they're going to be champions at fourteen, but most don't make it." He points out that Nancy didn't exactly leapfrog up the ladder of success, either. "She didn't win medal after medal as a teenager. She had some good performances, and some not-so-good performances. In fact, at one point, she moved away from singles, into pairs skating. And I thought, 'Gee, I wonder if this is a sign that she's not gonna make it as an individual competitor.' But then she did go back to singles. I was concerned about her putting all her eggs in one basket, but she sure did put in her time, an awful lot of time."

In spite of her punishing schedule and the ever-increasing absences, Nancy never let up on her schoolwork. That's a point each and every one of her teachers makes strongly. Bill Mucica taught Nancy's English class, in both eighth and eleventh grades. He was very aware of how hard she worked to keep up her *B* average—completing such required books as *Catcher in the Rye, The Adventures of Huckleberry Finn*, and *The Great Gatsby*—and was very impressed with the way she did it. "Nancy was the kind of kid who'd come up to me well beforehand and say, "I'm going to be away for a week, a week and a half, do you have any work for me?" I'd give her the work, and it would always come back done—and done almost as well as if she'd been in the classroom. In fact, sometimes better! In the beginning, I was stunned. Normally, when kids go away they come back with all these excuses about why they couldn't get the work done. But Nancy would come back with this *stack* of stuff. It got to the point where'd I kind of jokingly snarl, 'You mean, I have to correct all this?' After a while, we got into a routine and we had an understanding: I'd do my part, she did hers."

That sentiment is echoed by all of Nancy's teachers and others who knew her—if you have a job to do, an obstacle to overcome, you just do it. And if you work hard enough, you get what you want. There's little question about where Nancy Kerrigan learned *those* values: they reflect her hometown and her home.

Lydia Breen taught tenth-grade biology and has fond memories of Nancy. "I can still picture her with her short hair, brushed back in the style skaters wore in those days—and she always wore pants. She was very polite, very focused, and very responsible about getting her work done. Of course, she had a high absence rate, but there was never a time when I had to ask her where her makeup work was: she always handed it in before I got the chance. She'd come in after school to make up a test or a missed lab."

The science teacher agrees that Nancy was an average student, but not because she possessed just average intelligence. "Nancy took medium-level courses because she knew what her time limitations were. She knew she'd be able to devote just so much to her studies—the rest went, of course, into skating." Nothing distracted her from that passion, not friends, not after-school clubs or other sports, not even shopping at the mall or boys.

Nancy Kerrigan was not a star at Stoneham High School. She never talked about skating, and even if she had, the level she was at would hardly have impressed her peers. "It was never as if the kids at school knew they had a star in their midst,"

Thomas Ryan reflected. "Maybe she enjoyed some kind of acclaim within her skating circle, but here at school, she wasn't a public figure at all." Clearly, Nancy never thought of herself as any sort of special person. "Fame didn't hit her soon enough to make a big difference in her personality back then—she never received much recognition," Bill Mucica muses. "She thought of herself as just another kid. And for the most part, so did the teachers. I don't think that most of us knew she was going to be anything special. We sensed that the desire was there, though." Nancy never was a show-off, anyway. Head of the English department Pat Norelli agrees, "Nancy was just so exceptional in her humility. It never dawned on her that she was anything more than just a Stoneham kid."

Her near-anonymity at school wasn't only because she was often gone. By all accounts, she was the kind of kid, though incredibly conscientious, who was so quiet, "you hardly knew she was there." She was very shy, which isn't to say she was unfriendly or standoffish. "If you passed her in the halls, she'd always wave hello," notes Lydia Breen. She adds, "You know, we didn't have a chance to get close to her. The kid kept to herself— she was not an overwhelming personality. Nobody knew how hard she worked." Her ninth-grade earth science teacher Howard Dimmick puts it this way,

"She did not give herself enough credit for what she did."

Nancy's teachers agree on something else too—the naturally unassuming woman seen on TV these days is exactly the same girl they knew back then. "If you didn't know her, you might think the personality she projects in her interviews is fabricated, but everything about her, about her family, is very genuine," Bill Mucica says.

Did Nancy Kerrigan sacrifice any chance at a normal teenage social life for skating? There's no doubt about it. Few people remember her having any close friends or boyfriends, joining any clubs, or hanging out with any particular crowd. Her junior high school principle, Bill Orman, believes, "Figure skating, after all, is not a team sport. It's an individual sport. I think she made incredible social sacrifices."

Nancy's dad Dan has concurred. "We always told her she could quit at any time. But she always chose to keep going—even at the expense of having no social life at school." She had no social life on the weekends, either. "She realized she'd have to give up something," Bill Mucica says. She chose to sacrifice "weekends, parties, and fun."

She might have kept to herself back in high school, but it was *her* choice. Nancy always knew where she stood. Several years after graduation, she admitted, "I lost a lot of friends when I started skating because I just wasn't there. Some of the kids thought I was getting special treatment because I would arrive at school late and leave early."

Her teachers deny that they gave her a break academically. "She got the grades she earned," Bill Mucica states. "We showed her no favoritism. Not only did not one treat her specially, neither she nor her parents expected any special treatment." In speaking with some of Nancy's classmates, however, he found out what Nancy had sensed: "Some of them did resent her, but not so much because of perceived favoritism. They just felt that by being so conscientious, she sometimes made *them* look bad!"

Nancy's demure exterior hid a quiet confidence and determination. She never showed it at school, but her reaction to those classmates who resented her was, "I really didn't care what they thought. I just wanted to skate. It was an irresistible challenge."

CHAPTER THREE

Ice Teen: The Long & Short of It

The challenge was good, and expensive, too. As Nancy progressed from one level to the next—midway through high school she'd moved up from Intermediate to Novice standing—the cost of her passion escalated. Money was needed not only to pay for ice time, but also more and more for coaching fees, travel expenses, outfits, skates, and equipment. It wasn't long before Nancy's expenses eclipsed what the Kerrigans could even uncomfortably afford. Eventually, her yearly tab for skating—$50,000—outdistanced her father's yearly salary. "Danny's financial situation didn't warrant what we did," Brenda once confided.

The Kerrigans reacted as they always had; they

dug in and found a way. "It was simple," Dan Kerrigan said. "You work three jobs. One full time, and a couple more on the side." In fact, that's exactly what he did.

Even three jobs, however, wouldn't make ends meets. The Kerrigans remortgaged their home and took out loans that would eventually total tens of thousands of dollars. They relied on the goodwill of neighbors if Nancy had to be shuttled from one rink to another and neither Dan nor Grandma Mary was available. Money wasn't the only thing that was tight. Sometimes, Nancy had to practice in skates that she'd outgrown because she couldn't afford a new pair. If she complained, Brenda good-naturedly, but firmly, told her to "suffer in silence." She'd get new ones—as soon as they had the money.

The family gave up regular vacations—even their annual skiing jaunts to New Hampshire. As Nancy later told her high school principal, "I can't remember a single vacation or a time away from Stoneham that we weren't away because of skating." Her dad agreed, "The family hasn't been on a real vacation. We go to skating events, that's all."

Though Dan would never say it, he might not disagree too strongly with this assessment made by a family friend: "Her father almost put himself in the grave working to pay for her lessons."

As you'd expect, Nancy felt some degree of guilt about her family's support. As she told *People* magazine in 1992, "The sacrifices made me feel guilty. I feel like everything they did was for me. It's scary when they are spending so much money and you don't know what you will get for it." Indeed, the only hope Nancy (or any skater) ever has for a financial return on all those expenses is to become good enough to compete on an international level, go to the Olympics, and then turn pro.

Nancy wasn't thinking in those terms during her teen years—the money she might eventually make wasn't her motivation for skating. Her parents were well aware of that. So why did they keep up the punishing pace? Her dad admits, "I thought we had to be nuts, that we'd never stay in the sport. But every time Nancy would set a goal, she'd reach it. How could you tell her to stop?" Brenda Kerrigan sometimes wondered, too, but decided: "We just did it; I don't know why. It never made any sense. We just did it." Perhaps it was simply because they saw how much joy it brought Nancy—and overwhelming love for one's child never makes "sense." It isn't supposed to.

The Kerrigan closeness was never restricted to Nancy, Dan, and Brenda. The boys, Mark and Michael, shared in it, too. But it would have been superhuman for Nancy's brothers not to have harbored some resentment during their own growing-up years. While they have never publicly admitted to feeling cheated, Michael has confided in friends over time that every once in a while he wearied of all the attention lavished on Nancy. But whatever negative feelings there might have been, both brothers have apparently worked through them. Mark and Michael have obviously grown to respect Nancy's fierce dedication; today, they are simply incredibly proud of her. Michael continues to live at home and works at the Stoneham Ice Arena. Nancy turned to him when, in January 1994, she needed a bodyguard and companion.

It's sometimes assumed that because of her handicap, Brenda Kerrigan could not play as big a part in Nancy's ascent as Dan did, but according to family friends, nothing could be further from the truth. "The mom may have been blind," said Jeff Gutridge who's been covering the Kerrigans for the local newspaper, *Stoneham Independent* for years, "but she played a bigger role in the scheme of things than people would believe." Perhaps the biggest roles she played were those of morale booster and role model. "My mom became my biggest fan and my best friend," Nancy said, "She went to all my afternoon training sessions even though she couldn't see what I was doing. She couldn't read books to me or my brother when we were little, but she could do a lot of other things."

One of those "things" was simply to serve as a source of strength and inspiration for Nancy. Whenever the pressures of competitive skating threatened to become overwhelming, Nancy would no doubt think about her mother's daily struggles and frustrations. Just as Brenda has never allowed her blindness to stop her from moving forward and enjoying life, Nancy has also found the courage to push forward and find as much happiness in her life as possible.

Clearly, the bond between the two women runs deep. Nancy knew her mom would give anything to see her clearly on the ice, even just once. Whenever Nancy learned a new routine, she'd bring it home at once. "I do it on the floor of the living room with my arm movements, everything, so my mother can see it," she explained. If Brenda was in the stands at practices, Nancy would be sure to skate as close to the barriers as possible, in the hope that Brenda could make out just a little of what she was doing. Because darker colors are easier for Brenda to distinguish than lighter ones, Nancy began wearing outfits of deeper hues during competitions.

As she grew up, Nancy became more involved in helping her mom in practical ways as well. She shops for Brenda, helping her pick out clothes, and even applies her makeup. The two spend quiet time together away from skating. They go for brisk walks around a nearby lake three times a week. Both women explain their relationship in the simplest, but strongest, of terms. Says Brenda, "I'm proud of her." Says Nancy, "My mom has always been there for me."

No question, Nancy's success is due to a family effort.

As she grew, Nancy Kerrigan was starting to feel more and more at home in the skating rink. Figure skating—sometimes described as a combination of ballet, athletics, and emotion on ice—has been singled out as the most difficult sport a young person can tackle. It requires more time, dedication, money, and training than any other, if you want to be the best. She might not have said it out loud, but by Nancy's junior year in high school, that's exactly what she wanted. To that end, she trained harder and longer than ever.

She learned how to put together and execute the kind of routines that she would need as she advanced through higher levels. Naturally, she learned how to do figures. (That's where the sport got its name—tracing perfect circles, loops, and figure eights on the ice, and then retracing the etching exactly. Doing figures used to be compulsory in all skating competitions, but they've been eliminated. These maneuvers were as dreary to watch as they were to do, and Nancy Kerrigan was probably not sorry to see them go; figures were never her strong suit.

She learned about short programs and long programs; a skater who intends to move up through the ranks needs to perform both in competitions. All rules are set by the U.S. Figure Skating Association, the official governing body of the sport. The short—or technical—program is always performed first. It must be completed in less than two minutes and forty seconds, and within it, the skater must show he or she can execute eight specific steps, jumps, and spins. The short program is judged on both the technical merit of those eight moves (how accurately they were done) and the routine's overall artistic impression. It counts for one-third of the skater's overall score. The long—or freestyle— program is where the skater gets to demonstrate her artistry, athleticism, creativity, and interpretive skills. Usually performed within a period of four minutes for women (a bit longer for men), it must include a balanced number of jumps and spins, but because it is freestyle, there are no specific moves that must be performed. Since the removal of the compulsories, the long program now counts for two-thirds of the final score and is judged again on technical and artistic merit—composition, style, and presentation. The skater picks his or her own music to perform to in both programs. Scoring is on a scale of 1 to 6. The skater's final score is based on the marks she got for both programs. A top skater's scores usually range between 5.5 and 6.0—perfect.!

By the age of fifteen, Nancy had become a good jumper on the ice. She practiced and practiced until she could routinely perform difficult jumps and leaps—unusual for someone of her age and on her level. She was learning to do spins, laybacks, and all the jumps that top skaters have made famous, like the Axel, the Lutz, the Salchow, the flip, the loop, and the toe loop. (A definition of each is provided in the Glossary at the end of this book.) As a Novice, Nancy could do a triple toe—triple toe (two toe jumps in a row, each with three revolutions) combination already. She worked not only to learn new moves but to improve on those she had already mastered. Nancy always felt there was room for improvement. As much as anything else, that's what kept her going.

During her four high school years, Nancy advanced quickly through the skating ranks. She started off as an Intermediate, moved quickly through Novice, and was soon competing on the Junior level.

In 1985, during eleventh grade, she represented

the Stoneham Figure Skating Club in the New England Regional Championships held in Danvers, Massachusetts. Prior to that competition, Nancy was ranked number five among Junior Ladies in her region—but after taking the number-one position for both her short and long program, she moved up to number two overall. Since the top four winners in any competition automatically go on to a bigger event, she was among the skaters to compete in the Eastern United States Sectionals. That contest was held at a huge rink in Acton, Massachusetts. a place that would one day be Nancy's home rink.

At the Sectional Championship Nancy had the best day of her short career. She placed second, which put her in line to compete on a national basis for the first time ever. Although her showing there wasn't much to brag about—she came in eleventh—it was at that contest she first met two other talented young skaters: one of whom would become her best friend; the other would be forever linked with her worst nightmare. Their names were Kristi Yamaguchi, of Fremont, California, and Tonya Harding, of Portland, Oregon. Of course, at the time none of them knew how their futures would be irrevocably intertwined, but the three young women would go toe-to-toe on and off the ice for many years to come.

If 1986 was a pivotal year, it wasn't because Nancy's standings in competitions had improved; they were much like what she'd accomplished the year before. Still competing as a Junior, Nancy came in second in the Regionals (taking home a silver medal), but slipped to fourth in the Sectionals, which just barely allowed her to compete in the Nationals. There she once again came in eleventh. By comparison, Kristi Yamaguchi, an accomplished pairs skater as well as individual, was fourth.

But there *was* a big change in Nancy's skating career that year, one that possibly did more to set her on a path to the Olympics than anything she'd done before. She switched from working with coaches Theresa Martin and Denise Morrissey to the husband-and-wife team of Evy and Mary Scotvold. The Scotvolds were new to the Boston area, but old pros in the figures skating arena; former professionals themselves, they'd build a second career coaching young skaters to international prominence. When Evy met Nancy, he was impressed with her natural abilities. "She's very physically gifted," he said, "She has a strong body and was blessed genetically with a young, athletic body." Still, Evy saw lots of room for improvement. He described her style back then as "all inspiration with no technical stuff. She just sort of ran around from jump to jump without much polish."

It didn't take long for Nancy to appreciate the difference in the Scotvolds' coaching style—or its effect on her own performances. She agreed with their assessment of her style, too. "They have helped me a lot," she told *Skating* magazine, "Before, I could jump and do all these neat things on ice, but I had not idea what I was doing—like technique—I just went and did it. But now I have more of a concept of where I'm supposed to be and how I get to do what I do. I have a better understanding of what I did wrong or what I didn't do." Part of her new Scotvold-designed training regime took place off the ice; Nancy now incorporated stretching, sit-ups, and push-ups into her daily routine.

Excited as she was with her progress on the ice, Nancy still had high school on her mind. By dint of sheer willpower, she made it through her senior year with her *B* average intact. But while many of her classmates were deciding at which colleges to apply, Nancy had neither time nor a real strong motivation at that point to do the same. She had completed the courses required for college entrance, but Nancy knew she could put off higher education for a while at least—what she couldn't put off were practices at her new home rink, forty-five minutes away in Acton, Massachusetts. Long ago, she'd made the decision that her education was important, but skating was her life. So Nancy graduated with the other 250 kids in the Stoneham High School class of 1987, but, as one teacher put it, "She was part of the class that she graduated with, but they hardly remembered she was there."

With school responsibilities over, Nancy could devote even more time to her skating, but she also wanted to help out her family financially. She couldn't contribute much, but even her meager earnings from part-time jobs helped a bit. In the summer of 1987, Nancy Kerrigan worked as a waitress at her local Friendly's Restaurant and as a sales clerk at a store called Frugal Fannies.

The combination of the Scotvolds' coaching and having more time to devote to skating paid off handsomely in 1987. Though still competing as a Junior, she took home bronze and silver medals in the Regionals and Sectionals that year, and then she came in fourth, her highest standing so far, in the Junior Nationals. Kristi Yamaguchi came in second in that same competition. Tonya Harding, though one year younger than Nancy, had moved up to the Seniors, where, in 1987, she placed fifth in the National competitions.

Nancy's strong showing moved her forward into other types of matches. She skated brilliantly in her first U.S. Olympic Festival and won second place. And she traveled far from snowy Stoneham to make her overseas debut in the NHK Trophy competitions in Kushiro, Japan. Nancy came home full of tales of the Far East—and a fifth-place showing. She was on her way to international stature.

No one was more thrilled for Nancy than her parents, who alerted the local press to her accomplishments. Jeff Gutridge of the *Stoneham Independent* was one of the first reporters to cover Nancy Kerrigan on a regular—and very informal—basis. His office is just a few short blocks from the Kerrigan home. "I'd go over there to interview Nancy, and always, Dan and Brenda made me feel right at home. We'd sit on the couch, drink coffee, and they'd put on a tape of her latest performance. It used to embarrass Nancy, who'd say, 'You don't have to watch it.' In fact, getting her to answer questions was the only difficult part. No matter how well she did, she was just a down-to-earth person who didn't feel like a celebrity who should be interviewed, even for the local paper. The attention was so new to her."

Something else new happened to Nancy after high school graduation. She started dating. Nancy met tall, handsome Woburn native Bill Chase through her brother Michael; the two young men played hockey together on a local team. Bill was studying to be an accountant. He and Nancy started off as friends, but as the months went by, they became more romantically involved. As long as Nancy was around Stoneham most of the time, their relationship flourished. Less than a year after meeting Bill, Nancy admitted she was spending nearly all of her off-ice time with him.

Another important relationship began that year, too, with an Olympics-bound men's figure skater several years Nancy's senior named Paul Wylie. He, too, called Evy and Mary "coach," and soon the Scotvolds had teamed Nancy and Paul as practice partners. Paul remembers his first impression of Nancy—"When I met her, I was twenty, but she was just a kid. She was so far ahead in her technical ability, more so than anyone I've ever seen— and she didn't even know what she was doing." As their tandem training went on, Nancy and Paul became good friends and soul mates. He still remains one of her best friends in the world of competitive skating.

CHAPTER FOUR

Skating into the Bigs:
Triumph & Trauma

L ess than one year after she was a high school senior, Nancy became a skating Senior, passing the required tests to move into the big leagues of competition. It's from this select group that Olympians are chosen. If Nancy hadn't allowed herself to think "Olympics" before, by 1988 it *had* to be more than a passing thought. She entered five competitions that year and won four of them. In her first time as a senior competitor in the New England Regionals, she came in number one, bringing home the gold. Skipping the Sectionals, she raced right on to the Nationals. It wasn't her first nationwide match, but it was her first in a new league—which no doubt explains her only poor showing of the year. Up against such Olympic-level talent as Debi Thomas (who won) and Jill Trenary (who'd win the following two years), Nancy placed a dismal twelfth overall. It was Kristi Yamaguchi's first Senior Nationals as well, and she didn't do a whole lot better, coming in tenth. Tonya Harding's fifth-place finish mirrored exactly where she was the year before.

Nancy didn't let her disappointment faze her—she bounced right back to take the top prize in the rest of her competitions that year. First, she won the free-skating event in the National Collegiate Championships and then picked up two more trophies at international invitational events. She traveled to Vienna, Austria, where she placed first in the Karl Schafer Memorial Competition and then to Budapest, Hungary, to take the Novarat Trophy. Pretty heady stuff for a girl from Stoneham!

The Winter Olympics that year were held in Calgary, Canada—although Nancy didn't come close to qualifying (only the top three scorers in the Nationals have a chance), her friend and training partner Paul Wylie competed. Nancy cheered him on as she watched on TV at home, no doubt feeling almost as disappointed as Paul himself when he came in a distant tenth. But Nancy had already learned a lot from Paul, and how to come back from a public defeat was another important lesson.

Paul also showed her that there was much more to life than a sharp blade slicing through the ice, no matter how good at it you were and how good it made you feel. Paul Wylie knew that getting a college education was as important as anything he'd do in life. During his training and his competitions, and while he was working with Nancy, he was a student at Harvard University, majoring in political science. More by example than by anything he said, Paul influenced Nancy to go to college. It was something she'd meant to do all along, but skating alongside Paul pushed her to campus that much sooner.

So, one year after she'd graduated Stoneham High, Nancy went back to ask for her transcript and a teacher recommendation. She got the transcript from the principal, Mr. Ryan, and the recommendation from her English teacher, Bill Muccia. He remembers exactly what he wrote: "Nancy is the type of person you think of as having grown up in the Fifties. She has a very solid family who are very supportive of her. She's very highly motivated and never makes excuses—where do you find a kid like that in today's world?"

Nancy had decided to apply to Emmanuel College, a small, all-women's Catholic college with a top-notch academic reputation. She chose it for a number of reasons, not the least of which was its proximity to home. Emmanuel is located fifteen miles from Stoneham, near Fenway Park in Boston. Students from over fifty-five countries have enrolled there, and the average class size was smaller than at Stoneham High School—approximately twelve students per class. It was also the type of school that could working around Nancy's skating schedule. If she was able to fit in only a couple of courses per semester, or needed to take classes at night, it would not be a problem. In fact, Emmanuel prides itself on nurturing talented students who, according to a professor, "might need a little extra shove, or some extra accommodations with her schedule, or guidance in choosing the right courses."

Upon her acceptance, Nancy found she'd chosen well: Emmanuel was not only a warm and receptive place to study, professors there were more than happy to go the extra mile for her.

Louise Cash, who is head of the Department of Speech Communications/Theater and Music at Emmanuel, was one of those professors. Her introductory class, Dynamics of Speech Communication, was not normally open to freshman. But the school knew that Nancy Kerrigan was no ordinary first-termer. As Ms. Cash recounts, "One of the deans of the college came to me and said, 'There's someone you need to put in your class. I think this kid is going to be a star, and we have to accommodate her schedule. Your class starts at five-thirty in the evening, and she can make that.' " Timing wasn't the only reason the school thought that particular course would work well for Nancy. "She was very, very shy," Ms. Cash asserts. "She found it very difficult to speak to people, and my course teaches how to give speeches and work on your interpersonal communication as well. I'd remind Nancy, 'You have to learn how to talk to people because one day, you're going to spend more time speaking than you do on the ice.' " At first, the course was scary for Nancy. She was much younger than most of the other students there, and she looked it, because she often came casually dressed, wearing baseball cap and no makeup. In Professor Cash's words, "She'd come to class, looking quite literally like a little kid. She'd just sort of slink in and out." Nancy's speeches, more often than not, had to do with skating. Even with such a familiar subject, they were never easy for her. Her professor describes a typical speech: "She'd get up in front of the class, start to speak, then blurt out, 'Can I start over? Oh, I wish I could skate instead of doing this!' She was quite candid about her fear of public speaking. The class was utterly charmed. It wasn't only her candor, she just had this quality—everyone loved her. Nancy just naturally wins people over."

Because Professor Cash was also Nancy's freshman adviser, she got to know Nancy quite well—she became an instant fan, not only of the skater, but of the person. "Nancy is a very beguilingly honest woman. She is very shy, but she genuinely loves people. With her, what you see is what you get: she's very honest, very real." After Nancy explained about her background and her family, Professor Cash came up with this assessment: "Her parents believed in her and her talent. I think the strength she gets comes from that, the sense that people have always been on her side.

"Even back then, Nancy was not the type of person to say, 'Someday, I'm going to take over the world.' Instead, her attitude was, 'I'm going to put my best foot forward and just see how far I can go with this. I'm going to get better and better all the time.' "

As it turned out, Nancy's attendance record at college *was* quite spotty. She attempted to take twelve credit hours per semester, knowing all along that it would take her extra time to graduate. During certain hectic semesters, however, she could barely find the time to take one night class a week. "Keeping up with classes at Emmanuel has sometimes been hard because of my training and traveling," she has said. "But everyone at the college has been so supportive. They give me the extra time and flexibility I've needed." As she'd done in high school, Nancy was very dedicated about making up all her missed classes and assignments. Often that meant taking papers home. "She would do over and above the call of duty to make sure she got the proper credit and make up the missed classes. And she was very apologetic about it—she never thought she deserved special treatment," Professor Cash remembers.

In the end it took her over four years to do it, but Nancy racked up enough credits to earn an associate's degree (a two-year degree) in business studies. "It's not a degree we normally give," admitted Professor Cash. "We're a four-year college. But with the candid realization that continuing two more years on her schedule was probably not in the cards, we awarded her this degree."

Nancy doesn't downplay the achievement. She really does understand how critical an education is and uses her own example when she talks to young skaters. "I didn't finish college, but I do have a two-year degree. I think it's really important to know that school is so important, that skating isn't everything. I see kids so absorbed in it. Your body can't last forever, but your mind does. And even if you do go further in skating, that's not all people talk about. So you need an education."

Nancy Kerrigan's ties to Emmanuel remain very

strong. She's often photographed in her school sweatshirt, on and off the ice, and she's pictured in the school's official brochure. They send her bouquets of flowers in the school colors of blue and gold before every competition, with a note or telegram from Emmanuel's president, Sister Janet Eisner, Sister of Notre Dame de Namur.

During her college years, there was ample opportunity to send flowers. In 1989, Nancy entered six competitions and began in earnest to experience the real ups and downs of an Olympic-caliber figure skater. She'd never had a straight route to the top, but the next few years were a real roller coaster of fabulous flips and flagrant flops. She came in first in both the New England (Regionals) and Seniors and the Eastern (Sectionals) Seniors. It was at the latter that Nancy's mother was first able to witness her daughter's performance using video equipment provided for her at the site. Prior to that, Brenda had had to sit in the stands with the rest of the parents and try to picture the action as Dan described it to her.

Next, Nancy upped her standing in the Nationals, vaulting from the previous twelfth position, to fifth in 1989. Not quite good enough to make it to the World Championship, but not far behind Tonya's third-place finish, or Kristi's silver-medal second. Jill Trenary, of course, was first.

Nancy came up against Tonya again in the Skate America International match. Naturally, Dan and Brenda were in Nancy's cheering section—even though they had to drive for nineteen hours to Indianapolis to be there. Nancy ended up in fifth place, as Tonya took the gold. In the United States Olympic Sports Festival, it was her friend Kristi who skated into first place, while she settled—not unhappily, either—for third. Nancy then traveled all the way to Sofia, Bulgaria, to bring home the bronze, third place, in the World University Games.

Despite being competitors—and despite the fact that the girl from Fremont always came out ahead—Nancy Kerrigan and Kristi Yamaguchi (whose friends all call her "Yama") became close off the ice. Nancy described their relationship to a reporter by saying, "We've become good friends over the years. Competing against one another never gets in the way of our friendship. We are just doing what we have to do. She does her job, I do mine. We have no control over how the judges vote. We all support each other. [Right before she skates] we tell Kristi, 'Go out there and make it tough for us.' "

If Nancy has never had that kind of relationship with Tonya Harding, she *has* had a more even competitive record against her. For while Nancy, up to that point, anyway, had never beaten Kristi in a competition, she was on her way to topping Tonya many times, starting in 1990. By taking first place in the Olympic Sports Festival in Minneapolis, Nancy skated past her blond West Coast rival, who had to settle for the silver (second place). Although Nancy's fourth-place showing in the Nationals in Salt Lake City that year was nothing to brag about, it still outshone Tonya's lackluster seventh place. It also earned her an alternate spot at the World Championships in Halifax, Nova Scotia, where she watched Kristi earn a not-too-shabby fourth-place finish.

Other high points for Nancy that year included a gold at the Eastern Seniors (Sectionals), and third-place finishes at both the Skate Electric Challenge Cup in England and the Trophée Lalique competition.

There was, of course, more than one low point to the year as well. Nancy empathized with Paul Wylie, who sank to a humiliating tenth-place finish at the World Championships. She suffered her own dose of humiliation soon after at the Goodwill Games in Seattle. She wasn't even supposed to skate there, but she was a last-minute replacement for Holly Cook and, as one review mentioned, "She was probably not ready." Nancy toppled a total of five times and left the ice with hot tears of shame running down her face. Not only did she place just fifth when she should have done much better, but the write-ups about the event didn't show much "goodwill" at all. Said one, "It was traumatic for her." Opined another, "It was a disaster that might have ruined her career. She was more into beating Kristi (who came in first) and Jill Trenary than focusing on her routine."

Interestingly, Nancy herself did not disagree with some of the criticism. She has never been one to make excuses for a poor showing; she accepts the responsibility and simply tries to do better the next time around. "I heard Jill's marks right before going out there and I started thinking too much," she admitted to *Skating* magazine, "I thought, 'This is unbelievable; I'm not even supposed to be here!' I had it physically, but my mind messed it up."

Her coach agreed, "She was there, she had it, and just didn't know how to cope with it. The only thing that can stand in her way is herself. You have to learn how to win." For Nancy, that would prove to be the hardest lesson of all.

CHAPTER FIVE

Soul on Ice: "Wow, Cool, They Like Me!"

As 1990 came to a close, Nancy Kerrigan had set a new goal for herself: to qualify for the World Championships by taking one of the top three spots at the upcoming Nationals in Minneapolis, Minnesota. She believed she had a fair shot at finally nabbing a medal of gold, silver, or bronze in the U.S. Championships. "I missed it by very little last year," she'd explained, referring to her fourth-place finish in Salt Lake City, "It was kind of disappointing, but it's okay. I skated well, so I'm happy with what I did. I try to improve every year. In Seniors, I went from twelfth, to fifth, to fourth. Who knows, next year, hopefully top three. I want to move up!" And so she did.

Nancy prepared with a new training regime and a brand-new location. For most of the winter months, she'd trained at the rink in Acton, but during the summer, the Scotvolds moved her to the Tony Kent Arena in East Dennis, Cape Cod. The distance from Stoneham, about three hours, was too great for a daily commute, so for the first time in her twenty-one years, Nancy Kerrigan lived away from home. It was the perfect arrangement—she was not too far away from Stoneham, so when the "homesick" blues struck, she could jump in the car and be in the Kerrigan kitchen in practically no time at all. Otherwise, she could concentrate fully on her training and on having fun. She shared a house on the Cape with other students of Evy and Mary's, including her friend Paul Wylie, who tattled that he and Nancy got along even though, "I'm a slob and she's a neat freak" (no doubt from having lived with a mom who might trip over things left on the floor).

During her time in Cape Cod, Nancy practiced her jumps, spins, and laybacks, skating a good four to five hours every day. Not all practices were great. Sometimes, when she was having a particularly off day, she simply asked Evy's permission to practice a pairs routine with Paul—which, according to eyewitnesses, was a hoot. Nancy was learning that "lightening up" took the pressure off, and taking the pressure off led to better results.

In addition, she trained with weights and did lots of stretching. Jogging was out because of tendinitis in her Achilles' heel, but for fun, she and Paul would go biking and Rollerblading—even after the sun went down. "We Rollerbladed in the dark all around the Cape," Paul recollected in a *Newsweek* article. "I kept saying, 'We're going to get run over,' but Nancy was totally unafraid."

It was with this type of optimistic attitude and a fresh new regime that Nancy began 1991, which—with few exceptions—would prove to be one of her sweetest years ever on skates.

Her first accomplishment was to ace the Eastern Sectionals—she sailed right into first place. She also came out on top in the Nation's Cup and managed a third-place finish at that year's Trophée Lalique, which was held at the Olympic ice rink in Albertville. (Japan's Midori Ito took the gold; Kristi Yamaguchi, the second-place silver).

Then, it was off to Minneapolis for the Nationals. History would be made at that event, though not by Nancy. With the exception of Olympian Jill Trenary, who had to withdraw because of an infection, all of Nancy's normal nemeses were on hand, including Tonya and Kristi. Conventional wisdom had the gold, in fact, going to Kristi, who was the overwhelming favorite. But at the end of the day, a second-place Kristi cried inconsolably, as the eyes of the world were riveted on the daredevil from Portland, Oregon. For Tonya Harding had done something no American female figure skater had ever done before—she had landed a perfect triple Axel, and she spun all the way home with the gold medal. What did it do for Tonya's career? The write-up in *Sports Illustrated* put it succinctly: "In one energized four-minute free-skating program, Harding leapt from nowhere into history. . . ." Tonya's victory may have taken Kristi by surprise, but not Nancy, who said of her rival, "She's been working on it a long time. I figured she was going to hit it in one of these programs." Neither Kristi nor Nancy could land a triple Axel, not then and not now.

As for Nancy's own performance in Minneapolis, a spill at the beginning of a simple double Lutz during her free skate temporarily unnerved her, but she recovered and skated the rest of her program spectacularly. She got a standing ovation, a third-place finish, and the satisfaction of finally taking a medal in the Nationals. Even better, she had achieved her goal of going it to the World Championships. Who knew that, too, would be a record-setting, history-making competition? Certainly not Nancy. She was just happy to be going.

So were her parents. The 1991 World Figure Skating Championships were held in Munich, Germany, and for the first time, Dan and Brenda Kerrigan decided to accompany their daughter overseas. They'd been to every single one of her U.S. performances but had never been able to attend a meet on foreign ice. But this was the Worlds—and although forecasters didn't give Nancy much of a chance to medal, it was her first time, and her mom and dad were determined to be there. Without a TV monitor, Brenda wouldn't be able to see anything except a beautiful blur on the ice, but they forged ahead. Of course, it was all worth it.

At the 1991 Worlds, the United States squad turned in the single greatest team performance in the history of women's Figure skating. For the first time in the seventy-three years that women had competed in a singles event at the World Figure Skating Championships, the gold, silver, and bronze medalists were all from the same country. The women were Kristi Yamaguchi (first place), Tonya Harding (second), and Nancy Kerrigan (third). The results were so unexpected that organizers, who'd prepared just two American flags, had to remove a decorative third one from the Olympic Hall to use in the awards ceremony.

Kristi, coming off her disappointing second-place

finish at the Nationals, gave new meaning to the word "comeback." She skated flawlessly, landing six triples and earning her first perfect score, a 6.0 for artistic expression. She shrieked with joy at the announcement and proudly took her place as the new world champion.

Tonya, the reigning U.S. ice queen, was actually quite content with her second-place finish in Munich. "I'm really happy to be second. I'm not disappointed. I didn't deserve to win. I made two major mistakes," she said with refreshing humility, referring to an intended triple toe–triple toe combination that she had failed to pull off. In all, she'd landed only four of the seven triples planned.

The press said that "Nancy Kerrigan, the most lyrical skater of the three, looked the most astonished of all to win a medal." Maybe she looked that way because no one had expected her to win. And after her free skate, when she was only in fifth place, chances are *she* didn't expect to medal either. But the skaters who came after her flubbed monumentally. Surya Bonaly of France tried a quadruple jump but didn't quite make it—then she bellyflopped altogether. Japan's Midori Ito—alternately tagged "the Queen of Jumpers" (she's the first woman *ever* to land a triple Axel) or "the Michael Jordan of figure skating"—nailed only four of her eight triples that day and fell to boot.

In fact, Nancy fell as well. She had six triples planned and aced only four of them. But she impressed the judges with her delicacy and expression—and when those who skated after her messed up, she slid into third place. In the stands Brenda Kerrigan wept with pride. It was her, in fact, not Nancy who would say it out loud: "At the Worlds, that's when we started thinking that Nancy had a chance to make the Olympics." At that point, the games were eleven months away.

Between the bronzes—at the Nationals and now at the Worlds—Nancy Kerrigan had skated squarely into the spotlight. Journalists jockeyed for interviews; photographers begged or "one more shot." She was not comfortable with the attention and, despite her college course in public speaking, it showed. "Her press conferences consist mostly of shrugging, making faces, and giggling nervously," *Time* magazine rather unkindly reported.

As always, Nancy expressed herself best on the ice where she was developing a unique style. She'd never have a triple Axel, but what she did have was completely mesmerizing. The word used most often to describe her was simply "elegant." She had style, elegance, and grace; she was a "swan on ice." Paul Wylie called her a "beautiful, lyrical stylist." Reviews hailed her "elegant balletic line." Her coach, Evy Scotvold, proclaimed, "She's incredibly fluid. She has a marvelous sense of her body. She is very elegant, and people love it. . . . She's both artistic and athletic." Veteran skaters opined that she reminded them of the smooth Jill Trenary—athletic enough to do jumps, but also the embodiment of the classic femininity that separates figure skating from gymnastics on ice. To others, she evoked memories of the "more traditional skating" of the legendary Peggy Fleming or, more recently, Germany's Katarina Witt.

The same people acknowledged Tonya Harding's superb athletic ability—"Her jumping technique is probably the most phenomenal in the world, among men or women," as one reviewer put it—but her style on ice was described more often as "tomboyish" and "daredevilish." Never "delicate" or "elegant."

Even back in 1991 the lines had been drawn: Tonya, the acrobat-athlete who skated to the raucous music of ZZ Top vs. Nancy, the elegant ballerina who often chose to perform to classical interpretations.

Nancy had something else, too: "packaging." Her routine, became known for their interesting choreography, spins, and interconnecting steps. For much of that, she credits not only Evy Scotvold, but his wife, Mary, who, along with Mark Militano, a former Olympic pairs skater, was responsible for much of Nancy's choreography. Mary often picked out Nancy's music and helped put the routines together.

Mary also chose many of Nancy's skating outfits. Incredibly, there were times when Nancy didn't even know what Mary had chosen. On one occasion, Mary had seen a dress in the pages of tony *Town & Country* magazine. It was long-sleeved, gold-beaded, open-backed—and white. Mary envisioned Nancy accessorizing it with white earrings, a white hair ribbon, and, of course, white skates. Apparently without consulting Nancy, she sent the design to a dressmaker to create a customized skating outfit. According to reports, when Nancy found out about it, she was upset. "It's white—my mom won't be able to see it," she protested, knowing that Brenda did a smidgen better if Nancy was in darker colors. But it was too late, the dress had been made, and Nancy wore it.

Though Brenda couldn't see her, Nancy did look magnificent. But then, she always does. For by the age of twenty-one, Nancy had developed into a classic beauty whose looks were often compared to those of the young Katharine Hepburn.

Her future looked bright indeed, but for all the praise and laurels coming her way, Nancy also found herself on the receiving end of some not-socomplimentary evaluations. These were not about her skating. Instead, they focused on her perceived major weakness—a "fragile psyche." Critics decided she lacked confidence and was unable to handle pressure. "As a skater, Nancy Kerrigan has always been an enigma," said a national magazine. "Blessed with a solid, assured technique—high, ample leaps, a long, elegant line, and instinctive musicality—she is an erratic competitor. On good days, she medals. On bad days, she has lost her nerve and scaled down her program by simplifying or eliminating tough jumps." Dick Button, a TV commentator and former Olympic skater, agreed, "She's an unusually strong skater, but in other ways, she's fragile, not confident." Even Nancy's own coach, Evy Scotvold, admitted that Nancy often struggled with her confidence and that one mistake sometimes caused her to unravel. Whether or not Nancy agreed with this perception was not something she was willing to address—not yet anyway.

Her hometown newspaper editor, Jeff Gutridge, has his own theory on the whole lack-of-confidence issue. "There was some truth to it back then, but it only added to her appeal. Like most average people, she sometimes struggled with pressure. People related to that and liked her even more for it."

Nancy had started off the year phenomenally, which made it all the more disappointing when everything seemed to grind to a halt during an injury-plagued summer. She'd developed tendonitis in both ankles, so skating was painful. But not skating was worse. "I tried to skate several times in the summer, but it hurt so much that I ended up crying and going home." Not for good, though. By following medical advice to rest up and wear cushions and pads in her skates, Nancy eventually got better. By the fall, she was gliding on the ice again.

In September, Nancy Kerrigan went back to high school, this time as a favor to her former teachers and principal. Stoneham High School students run their own little cable TV channel, and when they asked their most famous recent graduate to be a guest, she graciously accepted. "It was at seven-thirty on a rainy Friday morning," remembers principal Thomas Ryan, who interviewed Nancy for the show. "It was really nice of her to get up and do this."

Dressed casually in a black-and-white V-neck sweater and beige pants, Nancy haltingly, but honestly, talked about her life since graduation. It was as honest a self-examination of Nancy Kerrigan as you'd find in any interview she had given before or since. Some of what she said was surprising. She admitted that she never watches the skaters who go before her. Instead, she paces backstage and worries about things like, "Uh-oh, I broke a nail!"

She explained what elements go into designing a skating program. "You want to perform to different types of music, while including all your required moves. You want to demonstrate as much variety as you can. Nearly everyone [at her level] can do triple jumps, but you have to do them with style. Spins have to be fast."

Asked what goes through her mind as she waits for the judges to pronounce her score, she replied, "You have no control over the judges, or the other skaters in the competition. You only have control over yourself, and how well you train. So you just sit there and wait—I never have any idea what they'll give me."

Critics who pounced on the "fragile psyche thing" might have been surprised to hear Nancy talking about how she really handles her "bad" days: "There are so many bad times, sometimes I get down about it. But I never thought I should quit. I just keep thinking that if I quit before I've gotten to be the best I can be, I'll regret it. My attitude is, 'Okay, right now maybe I can't pull off that move, but maybe tomorrow I will be able to.' "

She also detailed her intense training regime. "I pretty much just skate. I spend every day between nine A.M. and two P.M. on the ice—with fifteen-minute breaks every so often. I have stretch classes, jazz classes, ballet sessions, weight training. The emphasis varies from day to day, but the time commitment doesn't. It's several hours each day."

In spite of the amount of time she's always devoted to skating, Nancy never felt it was an obsession. "I leave it behind when I leave the ring," she told her high school viewers. "It's like a job, you go crazy if you take it home. When I'm at school (referring to her classes at Emmanuel) or home eating dinner, I am not thinking about skating!"

She was, however, looking forward to a trio of major events in the immediate future: the 1992 Nationals in Orlando, the Winter Olympics in Albertville, France, and the World Championships in Oakland. There were no guarantees that Nancy was going to even be at all of them, let alone do well, but all three were no doubt on her mind.

Before she left Stoneham High that morning, Nancy decided to pop in on one of her old teachers, Bill Mucica. She made a point of personally telling his class about the importance of a good education. Mr. Mucica made a point to his students as well: Nancy Kerrigan is a perfect example that "sometimes, hard work, commitment, things like that, really do pay off."

* * *

Nancy had other things on her mind as well that season, good things. For one, she'd become engaged to her boyfriend, Bill Chase. Nancy has never liked to talk about her private life, but her relationship with the young accountant *was* the talk of the town. Editor Jeff Gutridge confides that whenever people asked about Nancy back then, it wasn't about her skating: "It was always—so when's Nancy getting married?" Everyone thought a wedding was imminent.

Also, Nancy's financial situation had eased up a bit. Medaling in the Nationals had helped her get some sponsorships, plus aid from the U.S. Figure Skating Association. The rules were that all of her sponsorships earnings had to go into a training trust fund, with 5 percent funnelled back to the federation itself. Nancy played by the rules, of course, but did finally buy something for herself: a brand-new car.

As 1992 began, Nancy's focus turned to the Nationals in Orlando, Florida. Naturally, her parents planned to accompany her. But this time it turned out to be more of a struggle than usual. They expected coming up with the money to be difficult; Dan's getting the time off from work was not something they thought would be a hassle. They were wrong. His bosses at Atlantic Gelatin reminded him he'd already taken his allotted paid vacation time. If Dan Kerrigan wanted to go to Florida to see his daughter skate, he'd just have to take an unpaid leave of absence. Still, Dan and Brenda didn't think twice about forging ahead.

Because it was an Olympic year, the Nationals took on an extra dimension. There were three slots on the United States team for the Ladies' Singles Figure Skating event in Albertville; at least seven skaters had a good chance to make it. All would be in Orlando, but only the top three would go to France. Aside from Nancy, Kristi, and Tonya, other hopefuls were Jill Trenary, Holly Cook (who'd medaled at the Worlds a few years back), plus up and coming skaters Tonia Kwiatkowski and Tisha Walker.

This time, Nancy had a huge cheering section. Along with her parents and brothers were forty or so other friends and relatives from Massachusetts. If Nancy felt extra pressure because of that, it didn't show. Instead, she put on one of her best performances ever. She and Mary Scotvold had chosen the John Williams' poignant score from the movie, *Born on the Fourth of July* for her free skate. "The movie was so sad, but I'm not trying to interpret the movie. The music is sad but powerful," said Nancy. Her performance was just as powerful, including four triple jumps, one in combinations, and a total of six other jumps. After her by-now trademark spiral ending, the judges were unanimous in awarding her second place. Only Kristi had done better, finally grabbing the gold.

Third place went to Tonya Harding, but not easily. She was beset with problems from the get go. During a practice session, she'd caught her blade against a wall, causing a tendon in her right foot to inflame. Still, she refused to leave the triple Axel out of her program, and, although it was suggested, she *absolutely* refused to withdraw, remarking, "I would never pull out of a competition. I don't think that is right." Already, the media was calling her a "tough cookie." Tonya did tough it out, took to the ice—and promptly fell on her opening triple Axel, in both her long and short programs.

Still, in the end, the United States would be represented in the Olympic Ladies' Singles Figure Skating Competition by Kristi Yamaguchi, Nancy Kerrigan, and Tonya Harding. Almost as exciting for Nancy was finding out that her pal Paul had again qualified in the Men's Singles; he'd be in Albertville, too.

If the Kerrigans thought Nancy was in the spotlight before, that was nothing compared with the deluge after Orlando. Nancy Kerrigan, new media darling, found herself profiled in such prestigious publications as *People* magazine, *Newsweek*, and even *The Wall Street Journal*. "The phone hasn't stopped ringing since we returned from the Championships," Brenda said breathlessly, "It's all so confusing. We aren't used to this. We've become more cautious about what we tell people and what we don't—like our address." Like it or not, dealing with the press was something Nancy and her family were going to have to get used to. They could not have known just how overwhelming it would one day become.

With the Olympics only six weeks away, Nancy needed to focus and train ever more diligently. But in between Orlando and Albertville, she had one more public performance, which turned out to be another wonderful morale booster. In February, she was the special guest at an ice show starring Brian Boitano and Katarina Witt at the Boston Garden. Nancy, naturally, was a hometown heroine, and the audience let her know it. "What made it so exciting is that when I came out to take my bow, everyone in the audience was standing up and clapping," she happily recalled. "I thought, 'Wow, cool, they like me.'"

The rest of the world would soon enthusiastically agree.

CHAPTER SIX

The Olympics:
A Good Skate

"I Can't Believe I'm Here!"

*F*igure skating has long been the most popular event of the Winter Olympics. More than any other sport, it is packed with high, edge-of-your-seat drama that builds second by second and plays itself out before your eyes. It is up close and personal, nowhere more so than in the individual events where you can see the expressions on each skater's face. You can see who's sweating, who's smiling, who's making something so difficult look so easy. As an audience, we hold our collective breath when a skater leaps into the air—will she land it? When she doesn't, and especially if she takes a fall, a million hearts break for her. Mistakes are not only traumatic, they're costly. Going for the gold can mean going for the green, too, as a medal at the Olympics often guarantees big money in endorsements.

The Figure Skating competition in the 1992 Winter Olympics, held in Albertville, France, was different from all previous Olympic skating matches. It was the first year that the "compulsories" (which used to count for a third of the total score) were eliminated from the competition. Skaters no longer had to trace delicate circles and loops on the ice. Now the free skate, or "show-off" portion, counted for a full two-thirds. This development favored those skaters who weren't much good at figure eights, but better instead at interpretive skating—like Nancy Kerrigan, who gladly admitted, "I definitely have a better shot without them."

These particular games were billed as a contest between the "athletes" and the "artists,"—power vs. polish, the press had tagged it. In the women's competition, the athletes were deemed to be Midori Ito and Tonya Harding, both capable of hailing a triple Axel. The artists were Kristi Yamaguchi and Nancy Kerrigan. In fact, each skater in the competition was by turns powerfully athletic and beautifully artistic. They had to be, to get this far!

Nancy and Kristi were equally awed to be there,

although of the two, only Kristi would admit to having dreamed of this since she was little girl, clutching her Dorothy Hamill doll. Nancy would maintain that she only dreamed about "getting better, getting to the next step." It didn't really matter, since they both arrived at the same place, at the same time. And this time, ironically, neither was expected to capture a medal. Kristi, the reigning world and U.S. champ, was expected to enjoy herself and gain experience for the next Olympics, only two years away. In Nancy's case, the competition—aside from Kristi and Tonya, the field included Midori Ito and Surya Bonaly—just looked too steep for her to crack into the charmed trio of winners.

Both Nancy and Kristi arrived in Albertville in time for the Opening ceremonies, a full eleven days before their competition was set to begin. They roomed together at the Olympic Village, where all the athletes generally stay. Media types who didn't know Nancy and Kristi thought it odd that "arch rivals" would room together. But that only proved how little "media types" knew. For not only had the skaters' friendship survived all these years, it had flourished. When Kristi said she really wished Nancy the best, she meant it. When Nancy said she was prepared to be happy if Kristi won and she lost, she meant that sincerely. It might have been hard for jaded reporters to believe, but it was the truth.

Nancy has a philosophy about rivalries anyway, outside of her relationship with Kristi. "We're all there for the same thing. You go out there and you skate and then someone else goes out there and skates. We're all there to do our best. The rest is up to the judges. It's not competing head-on with somebody, you know?"

Nancy was no doubt rooting for someone else at these Olympics: her partner, Paul Wylie. Not only had he won a berth on the men's singles team, he was also the Olympic team captain. Nancy spent nearly all of her free time with him in those heady pregame days, bouncing between practices and press conferences.

Because most of the athletes arrived in time for opening ceremonies, they had several days to get to know one another, if not "bond." Tonya Harding, however, was not among the group. She had elected to stay home until three days before she was scheduled to skate her short program. It was a risky move when you factor in the jet lag a nine-hour ride from Oregon to France is bound to produce. Tonya claimed she never got jet lag. Maybe not, but something hurt her performances. It was noticeable during her first two days of practice in Albertville, as she struggled and burst into tears after one particularly hard fall. None of this boded well for Tonya and her Olympic hopes.

Meanwhile, Kristi was concerned about getting stale from inactivity, since she could only get one and a half hours of daily ice time before the event. To head off the potential problem, *she* headed off—to a different training sight a half hour away. There for three days, according to her coach, she did her best skating ever.

Nancy wound up with another problem altogether: she'd caught the flu! For three dicey days, she and her coaches wondered if she'd be in any shape at all when the big day rolled around.

There was yet another drama unfolding behind the scenes: this one starred Nancy's parents, Dan and Brenda. Once again, Dan was having a problem getting the time off from work. According to the local Stoneham press, he had to go to his company headquarters in New York and "plead" with his superiors to let him borrow on his 1992 vacation time, so he could travel to France. When an answer wasn't forthcoming, his fellow employees back in Woburn took up a collection to cover the Kerrigans' travel expenses. Nancy's brothers, Mark and Michael, were also sent to Albertville by the generosity of others. Their trip was arranged through the Celebrate the Dream program sponsored by the U.S. Postal Service.

Of course it was Brenda Kerrigan who most won the hearts and sympathy of Olympic viewers around the world. For who could not empathize with the pain of a loving mother whose only dream was to be able to see her daughter? Not see her daughter win necessarily, just *see* her. The image of Brenda Kerrigan, her face pressed up against a television monitor, desperately hoping to get a glimpse of her beautiful daughter whizzing by on the ice, was heart-wrenching.

During practices, Nancy would order her mom and dad to "stay right here, and I'll come by and do a jump right in front of you," and Brenda might see a blur spinning on the ice. She'd brought a small portable TV to use during the actual events, but CBS (the network that aired the Olympics) provided her instead with a huge TV monitor. It helped, as Brenda told a reporter and later, an audience of millions. "I can tell if Nancy falls; I can tell if she does a spin. It's made it possible for me to see one hundred percent more than if I was in the stands, but not the way you do. I can tell if she does a jump, but I don't know what kind of jump. I can never see her face. I never see her hand. I would do anything to see her. There are times when I say, 'Come here, I just want to look at you.' We get nose-to-nose, and I try to see what everyone else does in her."

So while the rest of the spectators watched Nancy from a vantage point in the stands, Brenda and Dan—who shared a house with Paul Wylie's parents in Albertville—made themselves comfortable beneath the seats, glued to the tube. As usual, it was Dan's duty to give Brenda the play-by-play. Not that she didn't appreciate the setup, but Brenda did bemoan their isolation. "As nice as it is being able to look at television up close . . . I feel we're missing something. We don't see people and that's a loss. It's really lousy for him," Brenda said in an interview later, about her husband. "It's much more fun being in a crowd."

"I just want to skate clean at the Olympics," Nancy had said to *People* magazine only a few weeks prior to the event. As it turned out, she didn't—but then again, neither did anyone else. February 19 was the day on which the short programs were performed. For Kristi and Nancy, it was a good day—they both performed flawlessly. Nancy wore a white matte jersey outfit done by New York fashion designer Vera Wang, a former figure skater herself. Nancy landed all of her jumps, including a triple Lutz combination, with ease. She hadn't scored better than Kristi and didn't expect to beat Midori Ito, but when the Japanese star replaced her planned triple Axel with a triple Lutz—

and fell—Nancy moved into second place. Tonya Harding did nothing to threaten Nancy's standing. Unfortunately, Tonya's triple Axel had failed that day as well—she overrotated and crashed, and was in sixth when the short program competition ended.

After the short program, Nancy visited the CBS International Broadcast Center where she confided to staffers, "I can't believe I'm here!" In fact, she seemed more excited "just being here, where so much history has been made," than about her super job to that point.

The next day, during the free skate, Kristi performed to the Spanish themed *Malaguena*, and nailed early everything she'd planned. She did fall during a triple loop, and then turned a triple Salchow into a double—but to her credit, she earned the judges' admiration by pulling herself together and finishing her program without further mishap. It was a brilliant spectacle, earing Kristi near perfect scores.

Nancy performed her free skate to *Born on the Fourth of July* once again. For this long program, she wore another Vera Wang creation, this one in a shocking shade of chartreuse. Although she didn't skate quite as cleanly as she would have liked—she dipped and touched the ice once, then singled two of her three planned triples—she still, according to one review, "lived up to her reputation as an elegant artist." Nancy had no way of knowing if her elegant performance was good enough for a medal, but she must have had a clue after Tonya again missed her triple Axel and Surya Bonaly fell as well.

It was Midori Ito that Nancy needed to watch. At first, it seemed as if the Japanese skater didn't have her best stuff that day when she missed her initial triple Axel. But, in what would later be described as the gutsiest move of the entire competition, with less than one minute remaining in her program, Midori tried it again—and landed it smoothly. That success moved her out in front of Nancy.

Waiting anxiously behind the scenes for the medals to be awarded, Kristi and Nancy stood together. "Do we have to say anything?" Kristi asked her roommate. Nancy didn't really know—she did, however, know that Kristi was about to be proclaimed the new owner of "la medaille d'or," the gold medal. Laughing, Nancy nudged Kristi to go out and claim her just reward. And true to her word, Nancy *was* deeply thrilled. Kristi Yamaguchi was the first American woman in sixteen years to capture first place in the Ladies' Single Figure Skating competition at the Olympics. And she was her friend.

In fact, two of Nancy's best friends came up

winners that day. As Nancy and Kristi stood in the stands, waving American flags and cheering wildly, they watched Paul Wylie give the performance of his career. It was a stunning comeback after Calgary, and won him a silver medal in the Men's singles.

No one seemed surprised when Midori Ito was named the women's silver medalist, but in at least one section of the stands—and behind the stands—there were tears of joy and screams of surprise when Nancy Kerrigan was announced as the winner of the bronze medal. It was Brenda, of course, who was in tears. "I cried when Nancy finished, and I cried when she got her medal," she admitted. "I cry so easily!" Brenda would also later admit something else—she hadn't really expected Nancy to win. "I don't know how this happened," she said. "I had her in fourth place. When I hugged her, I said, 'I love you, you did great. But oh, Nancy, I didn't think you did it.' "

If her mom was surprised, Nancy herself was not. "I've worked really hard for this. I've worked really hard to move up every year," she explained. Then she added, "This is the way it's happened. It could easily have gone the other way. It depends on that one day."

When all was said and done, American athletes took home eleven medals at the 1992 Winter Olympics; nine of those eleven were won by women. In the Ladies' Singles Figure Skating competition, American women took two of the three top spots, even though not one of the nine judges for that event was American.

On the third step of the victory stand, Nancy smiled broadly. She'd told reporters earlier that she had never set a goal for herself of "winning a medal." Just getting to the Olympics was enough. Besides, skating for medals was the wrong reason for skating. No one has lived that credo better, or more elegantly, than Nancy Kerrigan.

Nowhere in the world was Nancy more of a heroine than in her own backyard, and the folks in Stoneham looked forward to honoring their favorite daughter. Three weeks after the Olympics, the town planned a "Welcome Home Nancy Kerrigan Day" and threw all of its resources into making the Festivities spectacular. Coordinated by the Stoneham Chamber of Commerce, the tribute lasted a full day and night, and, involved hundreds of participants and tens of thousands of spectators.

It started with a parade, featuring a total of seventy-five different groups, floats, marching bands, antique cars, Lipizzaner stallions, and even a U.S. Airforce F-16 minijet; all proceeded down a nearly two-mile route that started at Stoneham High

School and wound its way through the center of town. Naturally, Nancy rode in the parade. Propped up on the back of a convertible seat, with her little cousin Alison Schultz in her lap, Nancy waved to the crowd of over 40,000 fans who lined the parade route.

An ice show at Nancy's old haunting ground, the Stoneham Arena, was the next event. The two thousand available tickets were sold out immediately. In fact, people had lined up for hours beforehand to be sure not to miss out. Local hockey teams put on an exhibition as did up-and-coming young skaters. Of course, it was Nancy herself whom everyone had to come see, and she didn't disappoint a soul, skating her mesmerizing Olympic program in a personal exhibition for the wildly cheering crowd of home-town friends, family, and fans.

At night, a Nancy Kerrigan social was held, and hundreds of Nancy's friends danced and partied until dawn. When it was over, Nancy gratefully gushed, "It was a lot of fun. I had a great time. It's a little overwhelming. It's great to see how many people are behind me, supporting me. I'm very thankful."

In fact, she was about to be rewarded in many other ways as well. For even though her friend Kristi Yamaguchi got the gold, when the Olympics ended, Nancy Kerrigan's star shone just as bright. It would all lead to a year of thrilling highs and crashing lows: a year of living dangerously.

CHAPTER SEVEN

Blade Stunner: "Some People Just Know How to Fly"

"I wanted to skate because I love it, not to become famous." Famous last words—Nancy's, of course. True, becoming rich and famous was never her goal, but right after Albertville, Nancy speed skated into a whirlwind year of publicity, promotions, endorsements, ice shows, benefits, parades, and appearances—on top of her regular schedule of competitive skating events. It was a year in which the spotlight on her had never been brighter. She was showered with offers, many of which promised a handsome financial return for her time. She was besieged with callers asking for favors. *The Boston Globe* crowned her "America's Ice Princess and Poster Girl." *People* magazine cited her as one of the 50 Most Beautiful People in the World, a real "blade stunner." She was on the cover of *Life* magazine.

It was enough to make her head spin as fast as her trademark ice spirals.

Everyone seemed to have a theory on why Nancy, only a bronze medalist, after all, was suddenly so popular. They were all pretty much saying the same thing—she's a natural. She's not only beautiful, she's wholesome. Nancy may not have been the most articulate person in her interviews and press conferences, but an adoring public—and would-be corporate sponsors—quickly "got" who she is: someone who genuinely believes in hard work, single-mindedness, family, and small-town values; someone who has not had an easy life, but who has overcome adversity; someone who had the courage to pursue her dream over all obstacles. She's a winner, but more than that, she's human; she's the girl next door who doesn't think of herself as a star, who's as uncomfortable in the spotlight as any one of us might be. A very attractive "package" indeed.

Nancy's coach explained her crowd-pleasing appeal in an interview with the *Cape Cod Times*: "She is uniquely blessed with great physical beauty, while also being a very aesthetic, ethereal skater. Watch when she skates, her face and eyes are always looking up to her audience. Very few skaters do this. Everyone in the audience thinks she's looking right at them. It has quite an effect."

That effect was crystal clear to everyone—with the exception of the star herself. She was possibly the only one who didn't "get it." Way after Albertville, she was still saying, "When I go out and somebody knows who I am, I think, 'How do you know?' Then I think of how they must've seen me on TV. That must've had something to do with it."

As overwhelming and unfamiliar as the spotlight was, Nancy didn't walk away from it. She reacted in a fairly typical, practical manner, admitting to a reporter, "The attention is not something I wanted. But it's nice. It's different. And I know it won't last forever, so you take advantage of it now."

Clearly, the big reason for taking advantage of it was the pot of gold at the end of this particular rainbow—and the new rules adopted by the U.S. Figure Skating Association that in effect allowed her to make money without jeopardizing her amateur status. In order to qualify for the Olympics— and Nancy had every intention of competing in 1994—athletes have to be officially amateurs. The definition of what makes an amateur had always been someone who didn't get paid for his or her sport. It was a pretty clear-cut choice: if you wanted to make money, you turned pro and said "good-bye" to the Olympics. But a recent shift in the rules now makes it possible for amateur athletes to earn some money from their sport—as long as it goes into a training trust. Further, if an athlete, like Kristi Yamaguchi, who turned pro soon after the Olympics, changes her mind and decides she'd like to try for another gold, she may reapply for amateur status. Claire Ferguson, the president of the USFSA, explained the rationale for the new rules in a press conference: "Everyone likes to see a skater get the laurel wreath around her neck, but the expenses leading up to it are enormous—so why not help them earn some money?"

That's why Nancy said, "It's starting not to matter," when she was asked about the possibility of going pro. She didn't have to—she could stay an official amateur and still accept the golden carrot sticks that were being dangled in front of her. Becoming wealthy for herself wasn't the motivation. But a lot of people had sacrificed so she could get this far; here was a chance to say 'thanks,' in a way that could really help. Best of all, she didn't have to become an actress or say and do anything she didn't believe in. She could choose sponsors who were already affiliated with the Olympics, or who promised to give something back to struggling athletes. She could just be Nancy. America loved her just the way she was.

With the help of her agent, Nancy began to consider some of the corporate offers. The sheer volume was overwhelming. "One thing at a time," Nancy told herself whenever she'd begin hyperventilating. The estimates of what she could earn were enough to make anyone, let alone a working-class girl from Stoneham, hyperventilate. Figures between $750,000 and $2 million were being tossed around as estimates of her earning potential.

Naturally, Nancy knew that any outside projects she took on would have to fit around her training schedule. She honestly thought she could balance the two and do justice to both.

The Campbell Soup Company approached Nancy right after the Albertville Games because she seemed wholesome and heartwarming—just as they portray their soups. Since sipping a warm bowl of soup after coming in from the cold was something Nancy did anyway—and since Campbell's has been tied to the Olympics for twelve years—affiliating herself with this company seemed natural. The company was thrilled to have her. "Nancy Kerrigan's all-American charm and her grace and beauty on the ice both complement and underscore the replenishing benefits of Campbell's Soups. We're proud to have her on board as our spokesperson," trumpeted a press release. It also quoted Nancy: "Soup is an important part of my diet, and I'm honored to serve as Campbell's spokesperson." With that, she became part of their "Never Underestimate the Power of Soup" campaign. The first of what will be a series of commercials began running in January. The concept for the ad came up during a "getting-to-know-you" conversation with Nancy. Kevin Lowery, Director of Public Information for Campbell's, explains, "When we first met Nancy, she told us about how she used to play hockey with her brothers when she was growing up—that sometimes, she enjoyed it more than figure skating." Presto! A commercial was born. It features Nancy practicing on the ice, doing some jumps and twists. A voice-over explains how she grew up eating soup, how it reenergizes her and replenishes nutrients. It makes her feel so good, according to the ad, that she's thinking of taking up a second sport— hockey! At that point, four big, bruising hockey players skate toward her. She gives one of them a hip check—and the player goes flying across the ice.

In addition to the television ads, Nancy was featured in a brochure created by the soup company with input from the U.S. Figure Skating Association and the American College of Sports Medicine.

Titled "A Guide to Healthy Eating," it's full of tips on diet, nutrition, exercises, and healthy attitudes. In the introduction, Nancy explains that "eating smart makes me sharper, both physically and mentally." The booklet also presents Nancy's favorite soup-based recipes—Broccoli-Cauliflower Casserole, Chicken Dressing Bake, and Shrimp-Haddock Casserole—plus a two-week sample diet plan.

Nancy did some public relations work for the company off camera as well. She was the star attraction at their year-end employee party, held at the firm's headquarters in Camden, New Jersey. "We had people waiting in line for hours just to get a chance to meet with her and wish her well," recounted Kevin. "Everyone in the company just loves her and is very supportive of her. People stop me in the hall and tell me, 'Next time you speak to Nancy, tell her we're all pulling for her.' We feel that Nancy is part of our family here."

Another offer Nancy accepted was from Seiko. The watch company had never sponsored an athlete before, but since they serve as official Olympics timekeepers, they were looking for an Olympian who fit their company image. In fact, according to Seiko VP of Advertising Jonathan Nettelfield, they considered several figure skaters—including, at one point, Tonya Harding—but in the end, they over-

whelmingly decided that Nancy Kerrigan personi-
fies "grace, precision, and beauty, just like our
watches." They approached her after the Olympics,
and Nancy agreed to appear in an extensive print
campaign advertising Seiko's Limited Edition U.S.
Olympic Team Lillehammer watches. A portion of
the proceeds from the watches will go toward supporting American Olympic hopefuls, which no
doubt made the ad all the more attractive to Nancy.
Still, she came across as somewhat hesitant during
her press conference to announce the Seiko deal.
Accepting a customized wristwatch, she said can-
didly, "I'm not sure what I'm supposed to be talking about yet!"

Seiko's Jonathan Nettelfield got to spend some
time with Nancy, who also agreed to make personal
appearances at stores, trade shows, and sales
meetings. He feels, "It's not that she's shy, she's
just completely unfazed by all the hoopla that sur-
rounds her. She thinks, well, this is just something
else for me to do. She'll just talk in a normal kind
of way, which is a large part of her charm. Athletes
become larger than life . . . I hope that never happens to Nancy. She comes from a great family. She
really doesn't come across as a superstar."

More big-company endorsements came quickly.
Nancy was one of a group of celebrities who ap-

peared in Northwest Airlines' "Some people just know how to fly" TV commercial. Though she had no actual dialogue in the ad, according to John Austin of Northwest, "She really seemed excited about the prospect of working with us, and of course, we were excited as well. It's a nice relationship, and we've been very supportive of her. She embodies the spirit behind the slogan, "Some people just know how to fly!"

It seems natural for an athlete to pair up with a sports clothing company, and indeed many were after Nancy. She signed a three-year contract with Reebok and shot a thirty-second commercial that celebrates female athletes who have overcome adversity. A perfect fit!

Along with other Olympians, Nancy joined "Team Xerox" for a deal that does not necessarily require her to do commercials, but she will appear on Xerox's behalf and speak with businesses, civic, and youth groups at several United States Olympic Committee fund-raisers. Xerox is the official Document Processing sponsor for the U.S.O.C.

Representatives from big corporations with deep pockets were approaching Nancy left and right, but so were television network and movie company people. Plans were under way for her to appear in a children's Christmas movie filmed in Edmonton, Alberta, as well as host her own television special.

Besides her new careers as spokesperson and star of TV commercials, Nancy performed in the nine-week Campbell's Soups 1992 Tour of Olympic and World Champions ice show, a star-studded event featuring the biggest names in the sport. Many of her fellow performers were familiar faces, including Kristi Yamaguchi, Tonya Harding, Paul Wylie, Viktor Petrenko and China's Lu Chen. A total of over 400,000 fans saw the two-hour show, during which Tonya skated to "Evergreen," and Kristi did an ice interpretation of "Pretty Woman" and "America." Nancy chose to skate to a potpourri of music, ranging from Broadway's "Miss Saigon" to the Motown sound of the Supremes. A little lighter than her Olympic fare, for sure! Photos taken behind the scenes on the tour, in fact, show her in a lighter frame of mind. Clowning around with Paul Wylie, she looked more relaxed and happier than ever.

The heat of the spotlight and her newfound celebrity didn't draw her away from her hometown friends and family completely. She might've been America's newest darling, but Nancy's nose was never in the air. When asked to do a local commercial for the Stoneham Independent Bank, she agreed. She also did a spot for a small company called Rink-A-Link. Nancy didn't forget the friends and teachers who'd helped her over the years either. She appeared in a Fourth of July parade in neighboring Wakefield, Massachusetts, and even visited her little cousin Alison's preschool to sign autographs. When her own home town honored her with a parade and ice show, she took it upon herself to send free tickets to her old English teacher, Bill Mucica, who was deeply touched. "It's nice to know you're remembered," he said sincerely, "and even nicer to see that her ego hasn't gotten inflated."

Among her peers at the ice rink, Nancy hardly acted the celebrity superstar. A reporter observing her training at the Tony Kent Arena on Cape Cod noted that she was very much one of the group, joking around and feeling at home. She'd determined that her new head-spinning schedule wasn't going to distract her from perfecting her spins on the ice, and to that end, Nancy trained as much and as often as she could. Working with the Scotvolds and her choreographer Mark Militano, she spent months putting together a new program, dancing to music from *Beauty and the Beast*. The routine was set to include seven triple jumps.

That program wasn't ready in time for the 1992

World Figure Skating Championships, but Nancy skated brilliantly in them just the same. They were held in Oakland, California—the first time in five years on U.S. ice, and the first time ever on the West Coast. It was kind of a "gimme" that Kristi would come in first—no Olympic ladies' gold medalist had lost the following World Championships in the last thirty-six years. When Midori Ito had to drop out due to illness, though, Nancy had a shot at the silver, but so did Lu Chen and Tonya Harding, among others.

Nancy did ace the silver medallion, but it wasn't with a clean skate. In her original (short) program, she turned a planned triple Lutz–double toe loop combination into a double Lutz–triple toe, and then fell. Later, she'd explain the mistake was caused by a "body-memory" lapse. She recovered fairly quickly, however, garnering this review: "She is beautiful to watch and powerful in her jumps. Kerrigan has a strong style all her own and her mental maturity doesn't allow minor mistakes to upset the flow of her overall program." It seems ironic that only one year earlier, critics had talked about her "Fragile psyche."

That year, the bronze went to Lu Chen, with Tonya falling all the way to sixth place. She didn't even attempt her triple Axel, but missed an easier step. Afterward, Tonya fired her coach, Dody

Teachman (for the second time in as many years, according to reports) and rehired her original coach, Diane Rawlinson.

Tonya and Nancy both did better in the first USFSA-sanctioned Pro-Am (professional-amateur) event—the Chrysler Concorde Pro-Am Challenge. The winner stood to go home $50,000 richer, while the skater who came in second would end up with $30,000. Nancy and Tonya were the one-two combination in that one.

Nancy debuted her new *Beauty and the Beast* program at the Sudafed Skate America event in Atlanta in October. She competed with sixty other amateurs from eighteen countries and took second prize.

For the same reasons that corporate sponsors found her attractive, many charitable organizations also lined up for Nancy's endorsement. She said yes to many of them, but really threw herself behind one charity that touched her on a deeply personal level: Campaign SightFirst, the Lions Club International's global blindness prevention program. As Nancy learned when she came on board, the International Association of Lions Clubs is one of the world's largest service organization. It boasts 1.4 million people from 180 countries on its membership roster and has been raising money to fight blindness since Helen Keller started the first crusade in 1925. The Lions have established most of the world's eye banks and thousands of clinics and eye-research facilities, and they have distributed millions of pairs of new and used eyeglasses to needy people around the world.

When officers of the club initiated the Year of Campaign SightFirst—its goal is to raise $130 million by June 30, 1994—they thought that Nancy Kerrigan might be the perfect honorary spokesperson. Nancy *was* truly honored. In that capacity, she will make several appearances for them and has recorded a public service announcement as well. She helped kick off the campaign's first intensive fund-raiser in Minneapolis, by giving an inspirational speech to Lions Club members. Her mother was by her side.

Nancy noted that she was very proud to be associated with the Lions, an organization recognized throughout the world for its humanitarian efforts. She applauded them for the mission they'd taken on—to rid the world of preventable and reversible blindness—and admitted that although blindness had affected her own family, until recently she had no idea how large a problem it is throughout the world.

"I know the day-to-day reality of this disability," she said in her speech. "When I was just a year old, complications from a virus damaged nerves in my mother's eyes, leaving her legally blind. For any family, including ours, that certainly means adjustments. You see, when skating became more than just recreation for me, my parents were behind me one hundred percent. They agreed to take on roles as constant cheerleaders and sometime coaches. My mom's support and encouragement have given me the drive to accomplish my goals—and she did it all without ever seeing me skate. Sometimes, I hear myself say, 'If only she could see me skate . . . just once.' Perhaps it would be a sort of payback for all she has done for me."

Nancy explained that Brenda's blindness cannot be reversed and could not have been prevented, but that is not the case with millions of others. It is those people that Campaign SightFirst is trying to reach.

According to Linda Ivey Miller, a Lions Club spokesperson, "People just went nuts over Nancy. They were very inspired. We had gotten some of her skating T-shirts to give away as raffle prizes, but people went nuts over them, so we auctioned them off instead. The T-shirts went for one hundred dollars apiece—and these are people who really don't have a lot of money."

At the end of her speech, Nancy introduced Brenda Kerrigan. The relationship between the two women was very clear to the Lions Club people who were at the fund-raiser. "Nancy is always right there to give her mom her arm, to make sure she's okay," observed Linda. "But at the same time, it's not at all a condescending relationship. Some people don't really know how to act around someone who's blind, or needs that kind of assistance. It was heartwarming to see that in this mother-daughter relationship, Nancy is helpful in ways that most daughters never need to be; her mother gives Nancy emotional support with her skating. They're great people. There is nothing phony or superficial about them in any way."

On the way back to the hotel, Nancy was stopped by a couple of autograph seekers, who said to her, "You know, you and your mother are such an inspiration to us. Thank you so much for coming here." Since Nancy came on board, Lions Club has raised $87.5 million for Campaign SightFirst.

To contribute, or to get more information about Campaign SightFirst, write: Lions Club International, 300 Twenty-second Street, Oak Brook, IL 60521.

Nancy's charity work was emotionally fulfilling, her endorsements financially fulfilling, but in other areas of her life, small problems had started to crop up. Her relationship with fiancé Bill Chase had started to unravel because of her constant traveling. Also bothersome was what was starting to feel like the constant intrusion of the press. No matter how many press conferences she gave or questions she answered, Nancy admitted she still felt ill at ease. "I get all nervous and crazy," she said. It certainly didn't help when journalists quizzed her about her relationship with Bill. Her mumbled response to "How did he propose?" was "I don't know—why?" To another nosy reporter who also asked about Bill, Nancy replied, "What does that have to do with my skating?"

Even her coach was beginning to get concerned that Nancy's celebrity status might start to overshadow other things—like her skating. "We can't let her get overwhelmed by it. You've got to build up her confidence while also keeping her feet on the ground. It's very easy to be overwhelmed, especially when you're kind of shy and unassuming. Nancy is not one of those worldly wise, streetsmart people. She's still pretty innocent. But she's got good fundamentals in her life, and that helps."

It was on this note that Nancy began 1993.

CHAPTER EIGHT

On Thin Ice:
"I Just Want to Die"

The U.S. Figure Skating Championships—the Nationals—are held every January. In 1993, the setting was Phoenix, Arizona, and all eyes were on one particularly bright star—blue-eyed Olympic bronze medallist Nancy Kerrigan. Immediately after the Olympics, Kristi Yamaguchi, the one skater Nancy could never beat, had taken herself out of competition by turning pro; the title of U.S. champ was finally free for Nancy to claim. She had set, the press said, "the newest standard for Figure Skating excellence, and was heavily favored to win her first national title." Winning, of course, would guarantee her a spot at the World Championships to be held the following March in Prague, Czechoslo-

vakia. Nancy found the public's high expectations a
heavy burden to bear. It was her first time as a
clear-cut favorite, a scary proposition. "It's definitely different being the favorite," Nancy allowed.
"There's . . . more pressure." Perhaps she hoped
that by acknowledging it out loud, she could "ig-
nore it on the ice, and concentrate on my skating."
No such luck. It seemed the old "fragile psyche"
syndrome had come back to haunt her.

Big problems became apparent well before the
trip to Phoenix. Nancy's training sessions in the
three weeks prior to the competition were the pits.
"Probably as bad as she's ever skated," Evy
Scotvold would proclaim. Nancy was missing
jumps, making mistakes, and becoming very dis-
couraged. It was a vicious cycle—the more pressure she felt, the worse she skated. Although her
coaches tried to reassure her that she'd be fine,
their encouragement seemed to fall on deaf ears.
Since reporters had been admitted to her terrible
training sessions, rumors of Nancy's shaky confidence once again started to fly. Some went so far as
to have her "tormented by the notion that she is a
celebrity," as if worrying about the expectations of
millions of strangers was causing her to slip and
slide.

Nancy was still the natural favorite in Phoenix,
but other skaters hoped to clinch medals as well,

among them Tonya Harding, Tonia Kwiatkowski, plus up-and-coming teenagers Nicole Bobek
and Lisa Ervin. The contest was also noteworthy
because of the inclusion of Michelle Kwan, then
twelve, the youngest Senior Lady to compete since
1973.

After all of the buildup, the 1993 Nationals were
one of the sloppiest—and strangest—ever. Maybe it
had to do with the paradox of ice skating in the
desert, or valley of the sun, because it seemed as if
everyone suffered meltdown in Phoenix. Who
would have bet that every single top American
woman figure skater would mess up? But one by
one, that's exactly what they did, none more pain-
fully than the skater who *should* have been Nancy's
closest competitor—Tonya Harding, or "the
mishap-plagued Harding Gillooly," as the press had
playfully dubbed her. She started off powerfully
enough but had to stop and restart when a strap on
her outfit broke. Tonya deserves credit for coming
back to perform a triple Lutz–double toe combination, plus some fast spins and a well-positioned layback. But then her entire performance unraveled
when she fell in two triple jump attempts and stumbled yet again on a third.

By the time Nancy took the ice, she was well
aware of what had gone down before her—

everyone! "All she had to do was stand up on the ice and she'd win," said one eyewitness. But this knowledge affected Nancy's performance, and not for the better. She started out surefootedly enough, opening her original (short) program with a triple Lutz–double toe combination, acing the required double Axel and polishing it all off with her lovely spiral sequence. It was in the long program, however, that Nancy nearly blew the gold. Performing to *Beauty and the Beast*, she opened with a strained triple flip and blew her triple Lutz completely, landing only three of the six triple jumps for which she'd been aiming. A "less than scintillating performance," it was still better than what the others had done: she took the gold, but didn't shine as brightly as she'd hoped. Young Lisa Ervin vaulted from fifth place to second, and Tonia Kwiatkowski took the bronze, followed by Tonya Harding in fourth—she wasn't going to the Worlds—and Nicole Bobek in fifth.

When it was all over, Mary Scotvold opined, "Nancy would have liked to have skated her absolute best, but it was hard knowing the situation."

What Nancy said was, "I've learned that if I fall in the beginning, I have to leave it there, and not let it snowball." What she really learned in Arizona, snickered a reporter, was that you don't have to be the best skater in the United States to win the U.S.

Championships, you just have to be the best that day.

Trying to put the best possible spin on the situation, the newly crowned U.S. champion left Phoenix with these hopeful words: "Let's just say I left myself room to keep improving . . . there's a World Championship still to come, you know." But it wouldn't be that easy.

When Nancy left for Prague, the way in which she'd won the Nationals two months earlier was all but forgotten. She'd succeeded Kristi Yamaguchi as reigning U.S. champ; now she was expected to emulate her old friend again and take the Worlds. Early write-ups pointed to her "meteoric" rise in the world of figure skating, and U.S. hopes were very much pinned on her. Once again, she had trouble living up to the expectations, and her training regime suffered. During pre-Prague practices, she'd always leave something out when going over her four-minute program—purposely. It could be a spin or a jump, but she always held something back. This confounded and frustrated her coach, who would later admit that training sessions had turned into "protracted arguments," a power struggle between coach and student. "We used to have knock-down, drag-out fights," Evy revealed. "She would not do a complete program." It defied understanding, because being difficult, especially about her skating, was so unlike Nancy. She'd always been such a perfectionist. She'd never acted the "prima donna," and she'd certainly never been lazy. But the situation had gotten so bad that at one point, Evy had thrown his hands up and turned her completely over to his wife, Mary. Both Scotvolds were very concerned that she'd yet to skate cleanly through an entire program during practice. If you'd asked Nancy what the problem really was, why she refused to skate a full run-through, she probably could not have articulated the reason. That understanding would only come later.

Although Kristi Yamaguchi ("It's weird not having her here," Nancy admitted), Tonya Harding, and Midori Ito (who'd retired) were not in Prague, the competition from other countries was steep nevertheless. France's Surya Bonaly was there, as was China's Lu Chen. But everyone was talking about the world's newest teenage phenom—Oksana Baiul, a fifteen-year-old orphan from the Ukraine. As the competition got under way, Oksana, who'd never competed in a World Championship before, wasted no time in taking the figure skating world by storm with her flawless performance. Charmingly, she claimed she did it by "listening to my skates."

In fact Nancy started strongly and led at the end of the short program, with Oksana coming up behind her in second. The true tale, however, would be told in the free skate. For Nancy, it was a sorry tale indeed. (Not that she had any premonition of what was to come. In an interview done between the short and long programs, a jubilant Nancy announced that being in first place was wonderful, and said, "I have more than just the jumps, and I think that makes a difference.")

But as the strains of *Beauty and the Beast* began and Nancy took to the ice for her long program, suddenly it all fell apart. "She appeared to skate in a daze," noted *Newsweek* of Nancy's weak performance. What went wrong? Just about everything. She turned her first triple Lutz into a single, then her knees buckled while trying to land a shaky Salchow. She nailed only *two* of her six triple jumps (Oksana landed all five of hers; Surya, seven) and made so many mistakes—including touching her hand to the ice and taking a step in the midst of a combination—that when it was finally over, she'd plummeted to ninth place on the free skate. Once all the scores were totaled and combined, Nancy had dropped from first to fifth place overall.

Nancy was mortified, and everyone watching, in person or on TV, knew it. For as she waited to hear the judges pronounce the scores for her flaw-filled routine, Nancy Kerrigan sobbed, "I just want to die!" loudly enough for the television microphones to pick up. It wasn't only that she'd screwed up her program. Nancy's heartache was compounded by the fact that her performance was the worst showing by the top American woman skater in thirty years. Nancy's teammates Lisa Ervin and Tonia Kwiatkowski also skidded, and statisticians quickly figured out that for the first time since 1969, no American woman claimed a medal at the World Championships. The men and the pairs skaters did nothing to remedy the situation, so the entire U.S. team registered its worst performance at the Worlds since World War II.

In some bizarre way, many seemed to think that with one bad skate, Nancy had not only failed herself rather publicly, but had somehow failed the entire country. Talk about a burden to bear!

A widely quoted comment made by her coach probably didn't help Nancy feel any better. Perhaps Evy was still stung by the problem practices, and no doubt he was voicing his own frustration when he commented, "She thought she was going to a coronation, not a competition."

As if all that weren't enough, the ever-present media scrutiny was turned up another notch. Some of it was downright cruel. One reviewer, trying to be clever—at Nancy's expense—snickered that the "beauty skated like a beast," a reference to her musical score. "Nancy Kerrigan stumbled through her long program," asserted another. They called it a stunning setback, a disaster, a fiasco.

It takes a rare kind of courage to even *face* reporters after that! But somehow Nancy steeled herself and, with heart-wrenching candor, she admitted that her post-Olympic career had really gone "from poor to terrible to horrific." Without trying to make excuses, she simply said of her latest performance, "My knees just weren't working. . . . I felt more pressure than I'd admitted and it affected me more than I thought."

Finally, those who believed the fragile psyche theory thought they'd been validated—Nancy Kerrigan simply did better as the underdog, when she was not expected to win. Put the pressure on, and she folds. Some suggested that the humiliation was so great, she should consider quitting. No doubt some skaters would have taken a powder after the browbeating Nancy took on and off the ice. But anyone who knew Nancy Kerrigan, her family and her values would not have believed that for a second. "She's no weak sister," Paul Wylie has said, and he's right.

In the end, it took Prague and the devastating lessons learned afterward to finally force Nancy to fight back. It was a wake-up call, and this time she didn't miss the bell. Dan Kerrigan expressed his daughter's feelings this way: "She never thought about quitting for a moment. She was mad as a bastard and more determined than ever."

Nancy realized that pressure was only part of her problem. In much more practical terms, she simply hadn't trained enough the year before. "I spent too much time on planes, and not enough time on the ice," she said. There was an obvious solution to that one: lace up the skates and get back on the ice.

"Obviously, I've hit a pretty big low," Nancy said finally. "There's nowhere to go for me but up. It's going to be hard, but I know I'm capable of doing it."

CHAPTER NINE

The Comeback Kid: "Some People Lost Faith, But That's Okay, Because I Never Did"

Sometimes finding the courage to face your own inner demons is the hardest thing to do. If Nancy Kerrigan had been afraid to understand and confront her fears before the debacle in Prague, she must have known she could not afford to deny them any longer—not if she wanted to continue skating. Evy, ever the blunt one, said, "She has a confidence problem, but [before Prague] she only half believed it. If she doesn't get the picture now, she never will." But Nancy had gotten it, all right. She took a few days to reflect on what had happened and came to this realization: "In some ways, it might have been the best thing for me. It made me stronger, more determined. Some people lost faith, but that's okay, because I never did." She was, however, "very mad at myself."

Evidently the anger fueled a fierce desire to fight back with every ounce of courage and determination she could muster. "Prague was no way to go out," became her mantra, and it pushed her back onto the battlefield. The plan was to "attack" on three different fronts: body, mind, and soul.

Getting her body into shape was, in one sense, the easiest part of the comeback plan. For hard physical labor and long hours were hardly foreign concepts. Nancy believed in it—she just hadn't done it in awhile. Returning to the rink, she simply jumped into sweats, put on her skates, and got back to basics. With the help of her coaches and choreographer, she started by putting together a completely fresh routine. If it all worked out, it would serve as her signature piece. The new four-minute free-skate program was designed for the upcoming Nationals in Detroit, where Nancy was determined to defend her title as the reigning U.S. champion—and hopefully prove, once and for all, that she was not merely "the best skater that day," but the best blade runner on ice, period. Since 1994 was an Olympic year, the outcome of the Nationals in January would determine which skaters made the U.S. team that would compete in Lillehammer, Norway.

Nancy enjoys a moment of triumph after winning the 1993 U.S. Championships.

Nancy at sixteen, just after she took second place at the 1985 New England Regional Championships, Junior Division.

Nancy moves with her usual grace during her preliminary programs at Albertville.

Nancy glides across the ice during her long program at the 1992 Olympics.

Nancy skated at a 1992 exhibition with her close friend Paul Wylie, a 1992 Olympic silver medalist.

Nancy is congratulated by her parents after her thrilling bronze-medal performance at the 1992 Albertville Olympics.

After winning the bronze medal at the 1992 Winter Games, an elated Nancy congratulated gold medalist Kristi Yamaguchi.

At the 1993 National Championships, Nancy skated beautifully and took first place.

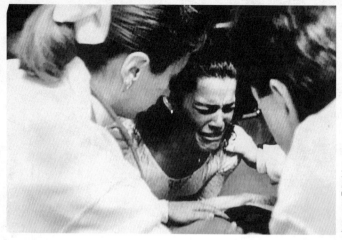

Medical workers rush to help Nancy immediately after she was brutally attacked.

"Why me?" a tearful Nancy asked her father as he carried her away from the scene of the crime.

Nancy holds back tears at a press conference just days after the Detroit attack.

In a fitting "No Limits, No Mercy" T-shirt, Nancy returned to the ice less than two weeks after being struck on the knee.

Nancy Kerrigan

Nancy raises her arms in triumph after finishing her first public practice since being injured.

Nancy was determined to prove that she deserved to be one of those skaters.

The music for her new program was a medley of Neil Diamond tunes, plus original melodies by Mark Militano; Mary Scotvold was the chief choreographer. Nancy was excited about it. The program itself was tougher than anything she'd ever attempted before. In addition to detailed combination steps and fast spins, it included a total of six triple jumps. Once she learned the program, she would need to concentrate on maintaining consistency and improving her spins.

Putting in more ice time was first on the agenda. In the year after the Olympics in Albertville, she had tried to train two hours a day, five days a week, but only when she wasn't flying around the country for commercials, appearances, and benefits, that is. Her new regime upped the ante: she'd now spend three hours a day, six days a week on skates. As for all those other commitments, most went out the window. One thing Nancy must have been able to see clearly was that she'd been wrong after all— she just couldn't balance fast-paced lifestyle with a down-to-earth, rigorous training routine. So although her schedule of appearances had been set for the entire upcoming year—"I got even more offers *after* Prague," Nancy said incredulously—she canceled as many as possible. Some of what went by the wayside—a cameo role in a children's movie called *Ted E. Bear, Esquire*, her own Christmas television special, and a party in her honor hosted by *Cosmopolitan* magazine. No time for any of that now.

Next, Nancy decided to borrow a training technique that her friend Paul Wylie swore by. "I learned to train in a more rigorous way," is how Nancy put it. In fact it was as punishing a workout as any figure skater employs—she would skate through her entire four-minute-plus program, and then, without taking a break, rewind the music, press "play," and do the entire thing all over again. This back-to-back blade running required Nancy to do twelve triple jumps in under ten minutes—an amazing feat, and one that requires huge reserves of stamina and mental energy. Yet, she did it every time, no matter what. And this time, she left nothing out. "I wouldn't let myself skip anything now," Nancy announced. "I didn't want to get into that habit." On one particularly ambitious occasion, Nancy swung for the fences, skating her routine *three* consecutive times. "And I hit seventeen of eighteen triple jumps," she said proudly. After that, going through it once would seem easy! Which, of course, is the point.

As Paul Wylie has described it, this technique is challenging physically *and* mentally. After going through a strenuous routine the first time, "You're dog-tired, sweating, pulse-pounding. By the second time, your fingertips tingle, and your arms start to fall. You've just climbed the mountain—now, you have to climb it again. In competition you can say, 'Okay, I can do this. I can do it at 80 percent power. I've done it.' "

Her efforts bore immediate results. Nancy had taken off several pounds and was skating better than ever. All of this work didn't fail to impress her coaches. Evy said, "She skated her entire free program without a glitch. In eight years, I'd never seen it before." Mary marveled. "She's never worked this hard before. She's never done the run-throughs she's doing now, double run-throughs, going for a perfect run-through. She's in fantastic shape. Her power is incredible. When she skates, she looks like she needs a bigger ice surface."

Even Nancy herself was impressed. "I don't think I ever knew what hard work was before! But I'm more relaxed each time I go through the program. For me, that's real important."

If training her body was something familiar to Nancy, strengthening her emotional state was not. But if she was to overcome her "confidence" problem, she must have known that the next step of her comeback had to happen in her head. Nancy had never gone for psychotherapy before, but sometimes growth requires exploring new ways to help yourself, no matter how scary they seem at first. She began to meet with a Boston-area sports psychologist named Cindy Adams. Officially, the reason was to "sharpen her competitive focus." What Nancy got out of her therapy, however, was quite a bit more. It was as positive as anything she learned from her new training technique. In fact, it was mind-blowing.

Nancy learned what made her tick—and stop ticking, too—and she was brave enough to share her very private realizations with the public.

After several months of therapy, Nancy had come to an astonishing understanding—her reluctance to go through her entire program during those problematic pre-Prague training sessions had nothing to do with stubbornness, arrogance, or laziness. It was all about fear. "I was really afraid to put my music on," she'd later confess to *People* magazine. "If I wasn't perfect, I'd get at myself, put myself down." In other interviews, she elaborated: "I was really afraid to find out that maybe I couldn't do it. It's kind of scary, giving everything you have. What if [you find out] you're not as good as you think you are?" Nancy Kerrigan had come to a point in her career where she doubted her own talent. Facing that self-doubt, articulating it, and choosing to combat it in the most public of ways: that's real courage.

Nancy reached another explosive conclusion—sometime over the past two years her motivation for competing had shifted. She no longer skated to win, but instead she skated *not to lose*. She was driven more by fear of failure than by the heady anticipation of success.

Nancy found that working on emotional issues is just as time-consuming, and in its own way, as difficult, as physical training. "I had to work every day at getting over being negative," she shared. "If I miss my first triple jump, I have to say, 'All right, there's a lot more to my program than one jump.'" And although she could finally admit that being the underdog had been a comfortable place for her mentally—"I'm a fighter and it's easier for me to fight my way back than to start at the top," she'd once said—she could cope with being the top dog, too. When asked about her chances at Lillehammer, Nancy confidently told reporters that she truly believed she'd do just fine. She was really looking forward to proving it.

Nancy credited her work with the sports psychologist for her new optimistic attitude. "It's helped a lot, I've never been so positive. I feel everything is going well."

The third "front" of Nancy's comeback battle was even more personal. As a popular Billy Joel song put it, "It's all about soul," and Nancy started replenishing her soul by doing things that just made her feel good. That led her back to her family, with whom she spent more time than she had in the past year and a half. She took longer, more frequent walks with her mom. When Dan Kerrigan had to have back surgery, Nancy was there for him, sometimes accompanying him on his nightly therapeutic walks. She hung out with her brothers, and even played a little street hockey with them now and again.

There was some closure in her life during this period, too: some expected, some not. Sadly, Nancy's grandmother Mary passed away; the entire family pulled together for support and comfort during the rough weeks before and after her death. And Nancy had to finally admit that her relationship with Bill Chase just wasn't working. They'd gotten engaged but could never find the time to be together, let alone make wedding plans. The rollercoaster ride of emotional ups and downs had to be over, so they broke up.

She developed some positive new habits during this time. Nancy began to do more soothing stretching exercises and learned a relaxing backstage technique to use during the wait before her turn to skate. Instead of pacing, fretting, and worrying about breaking a nail—as she'd told Stoneham high school students during her 1991 interview—she now put on headphones and listened to the music she'd be performing to, relaxing and visualizing each step of her program. In her head, of course, each step was executed perfectly.

Nancy did something else for her soul: she learned to lighten up! She spent more time doing things that made her laugh and catered to her silly side, like listening to tapes of radio station gag calls. "It helps to smile," she explained. "I know it sounds corny, but smiling makes you feel lighter. I think my routine in Prague wouldn't have looked so bad if people hadn't seen the horrified expression on my face." That Nancy could even half joke about the disaster was a sure sign she was getting better by the moment. In fact, she was even starting to get annoyed by the people who continued to harp on Prague. "Everyone keeps talking about it," she said, exasperation in her voice. "It's like, get *over* it! *I'm* over it."

To prove just that, Nancy returned to the public ice arena—with a vengeance. Her first time out, barely a month after the disaster in Prague, was terrifying. The media thought she'd made a fool of herself on national television and everyone had seen her all timid and teary, but now, the time had come to go out and skate in public again. Her first event, the Tour of World and Olympic Figure Skating Champions, was not a competition, and that may have taken some of the pressure off. Admitting she was scared also helped: "It was tough to go out in front of people and skate," she confessed. Happily, however, she skated well and her worst fears were never realized; instead, her bravery was rewarded. "It really worked out well," she said with a sigh of relief. "The reaction from the crowd was incredibly supportive. I said, 'Oh, good. They haven't given up on me.' Because *I* haven't given up on me."

Getting back into competition would prove a bit dicier. Her first competitive post-Prague event was the Hershey Kisses Pro-Am Challenge in Los Angeles. Testing her newfound confidence in an actual meet for the first time, Nancy started out strongly enough, but fell three separate times during her long program. The spills cost her the championship purse of $50,000 (which went to former Olympian Caryn Kadavy), but Nancy certainly skated well enough to take second place, and a not-too-shabby $30,000. Far more important than the money, however, was just getting out there and competing. By doing so, she took another big step toward proving that she'd reclaimed her confidence and hadn't folded. She proved that even more forcefully at her next Pro-Am challenge in Philadelphia, where she smoothly skated into first place without mishap.

By late fall, Nancy was ready to publicly debut her new program, the one she'd spent so many months working on with Evy, Mary, and Mark. Her next competition, called the Piruetten, took on extra significance because of its location—the Olympic rink in Hamar, Norway. If skating her new program in a meet for the first time *and* skating it at the Olympic rink put extra pressure on Nancy—so what? She knew she could handle it. As the Neil Diamond medley filled the arena, Nancy performed the way she now knew she could; she landed five (of a planned six) triple jumps, and earned six artistic marks of 5.9—nearly perfect. She placed second in the technical (short) program and first in the free skate (long); the combination led to a first-prize trophy. Her victory was especially sweet, for she'd beaten three out of the four skaters who'd leapt over her in Prague, everyone except Oksana Baiul, who wasn't there. "It felt great!" Nancy enthusiastically told reporters afterward. "When doesn't it feel great to win? I was pretty excited and really confident. I'd been training hard, and I felt ready to compete."

Nancy's new confidence extended to the way she was dealing with the press—less hesitantly, less modestly, and more articulately. When asked to forecast her own Olympic outlook, she said (for her) boldly, "Well, I've competed against all the contenders except Oksana, and I beat them all. With all the work I've done, I feel I'm good enough to win. I *know* it. Last year, I thought it, but I wasn't *really* sure."

Bullish on her prospects, too, were the Scotvolds, who said, "She is totally focused. We don't have to push her, and the training has made her realize how good she can be. She never knew that before."

No one believed in Nancy's ability to come back more than Paul Wylie. The inspiration she drew from him didn't necessarily come from anything he said: Nancy only had to remember Paul's stunning comeback in Albertville after a humiliating defeat in Calgary four years earlier. In skating circles and in the press, Paul had been dismissed as a "has been"; he'd even been denied a spot at the World Championships based on his past performances. In Albertville Paul proved that not only can you come back, but you can do it with style and integrity. You only needed the courage to try.

And so it was with that mind-set, with so many people in her corner, that Nancy was primed and ready to face the new year. She was going to show the world that she'd come back. Not only that, she felt it was crucial to erase the memory of the humiliation in Prague once and for all. "I just wanted to show everybody that I didn't lose it last year. It was just a bad four minutes," she said. Talking in December about the upcoming Nationals, Nancy told *Skating* magazine, "I'm going to be ready. I've put a lot of effort into this." Then, in what would later take on an ominous feel, she added, "Even if something happens, I'll know I gave it everything I have. In the past, that was scary. But this time, whatever I get, whatever I do, I'll be happy." She was talking about the possibility of making a mistake on the ice in Detroit. She couldn't have forecast that she would never even get the chance to skate.

In Nancy's mind, everything was set. It was full steam ahead. First stop: Detroit and the Nationals. Second stop: Lillehammer and the gold. Who knew there'd be an emergency—one that threatened to derail her entire career—in between? In fact, several people did know, but Nancy Kerrigan and all those who loved her were not among them.

CHAPTER TEN

Disaster in Detroit: "Why Me?"

*I*t happened without warning, and on the surface, without motive, a random act of senseless violence. There was Nancy Kerrigan, one minute talking optimistically with a reporter, a bright smile lighting up her beautiful face; the next, crumpled over, grabbing her knee, that same face twisted in an ugly grimace, distorted by agonizing pain and fear. She was no longer talking, but shrieking in a tortured voice ultimately heard round the world, "Why me? Why me? Why now?" This image would be immortalized, splashed across the front pages of newspapers and magazines, leading off the nightly news on every television station.

It was 2:35 in the afternoon on Thursday, January 6, 1994, and the Nationals were set to start the next day. Nancy, like many other competitors, was finishing her practice at Detroit's Cobo Hall. Dressed in skating whites, she'd just completed a strenuous session. She was off the ice, heading toward her dressing room, and had stopped momentarily to talk to a reporter. The backstage area was bustling with activity and heady anticipation. Although Nancy had been the last one to leave the ice, other skaters were still there. So were Dan and Brenda Kerrigan, along with a bunch of reporters, plus the coaches and families of the other competitors.

And so was someone else, someone with no legitimate reason for being there, except for the heinous mission he was about to carry out. He was dressed in black—black hat and black leather jacket. Sweating and jittery, he didn't look as if he really belonged there, but no one stopped him. He was after unsuspecting prey—only he wasn't quite sure which of the women was his target. So he stopped to ask a man who looked like he might know. "Is that Nancy Kerrigan?" the stalker asked, pointing to the unsuspecting skater. Frank Carroll, the coach of thirteen-year-old figure skating phenom Michelle Kwan, innocently replied that it was.

The man in black made a beeline for Nancy, who was still talking to the reporter. Both women had their backs to the attacker; they never saw his face. It seems that no one else did either, for afterward the police got wildly different descriptions. Running, he pushed his way in between Nancy and the reporter, and without stopping, whipped a black telescoping metal club out from under his jacket. With all the power he could muster, he swung the weapon, aiming for what he must have thought was Nancy's right knee. It was a direct hit, but not exactly on target—he bludgeoned the U.S. Figure Skating champion a fraction of an inch above the knee. The blow was so loud, it could be heard out by the rink.

All hell broke loose. Nancy went down immediately, her tortured, bloodcurdling cries for help reverberating down the hallway, bouncing off the walls. "Why me? Why me? Why now? Help me! It hurts so bad! Please help me!" She'd barely gotten the first syllable out of her mouth when Dan Kerrigan bolted, brushing aside spectators and even his wife—no one moves faster or with more urgency than a parent rushing to his injured child's side. In a flash, without giving a thought to his own fragile, just-operated-on back, he scooped Nancy up in his arms and ran for help. Clutching him, her tear-stained face buried in his neck, Nancy continued to cry out, "It hurts, Dad. I'm so scared. Why me? Why now? Why?" To all the world, she looked like a child, senselessly and viciously attacked, helplessly clinging to the support she'd always relied on, her father. "I just kept crying," Nancy admitted. For that split second in time, understandably, all her hard-won confidence and bravado were gone. So, too, perhaps, was her life's work.

Dan Kerrigan wasn't the only one on the run. So were the security guards, and so was the attacker. Fleeing—in the opposite direction—with just as much heart-pounding urgency as Dan, he headed for an exit, any exit. Panicking when he found a locked door in his path, he smashed through a Plexiglas partition to make his getaway, leaving the guards with a cold trail. Only a few seconds had passed. As Dan found Nancy a medic, the assailant ditched his weapon in a dumpster and sped off in his getaway car.

And so the journey for both sides had begun. Nancy's path was an uphill road to recovery; the man in black, along with his cohorts, was going down.

At the hospital, doctors huddled around Nancy, attempting to assess the damage and decide on a course of action. They could immediately tell that she'd sustained a severe bruise on the kneecap and quadriceps tendon; the area around the badly strained knee had already started to swell. As they waited, neither of Nancy's parents was thinking about her skating career. As Brenda would later tearfully tell a television audience, her only thoughts at that moment were, "Will she walk? Will she be, you know ... *okay*?"

Nancy Kerrigan, however, *was* thinking about skating. Less than two hours after the attack she was back in her hotel room, and amazingly, she had regained her composure. She spoke to a crew from ABC Sports (who were airing the Championships), telling them, "I just don't want to lose faith in a lot of people. It was just one bad guy, and I'm sure there's others ... but not everybody is like that." Clearly, neither Nancy nor her parents had any reason to believe that the attack was anything more than the work of a deranged stalker.

Nancy had also calmed down sufficiently to beg for the chance to compete even though she'd been bludgeoned on her right leg, the one she uses for takeoffs and landings. Though still in pain, she honestly believed she could do it. Perhaps she thought that, just by wanting to skate so badly, she could will the wound to be superficial. But her bravery was no match for the reality of the beating she'd taken. By that evening, the swelling around her right knee had increased alarmingly. The next day, January 7, it had shifted from the front to the back of her knee, and Nancy could barely bend her leg. A team of orthopedic surgeons gave her a local anesthetic and drained twenty cubic centimeters of blood from her kneecap. Afterward, Nancy tried to hop on her right leg, but she couldn't do it. She had no control. The Detroit doctors rendered their opinion—defending champ Nancy Kerrigan could not possibly compete in the U.S. Figure Skating Championships because of "pain, lack of motion in the knee, and lack of strength."

When she heard that, Nancy said, "I cried and cried. I'm pretty upset and angry that someone would do this, but I'm trying to keep up my spirits." Her tears, however, were not a sign of weakness, just an honest expression of real emotion. What were her real emotions the *next* day as she sat, stone-faced, in a skybox at the Joe Louis Arena—provided by Detroit Red Wing owner Mike Ilitch—watching Tonya Harding take what was rightfully hers? Photos don't provide much of a clue. They show a composed Nancy Kerrigan, little cousin Alison Schultz in her lap, looking down at the action on the ice. After a flawless and powerful performance, Tonya was crowned the new United States Ladies' Figure Skating Champion, and she'd be one of two women to represent her country at the 1994 Olympics in Lillehammer. The second spot was about to be awarded to the brilliant young Michelle Kwan, who turned in a mesmerizing silver-medaling performance.

But the hearts of USFSA officials—and the hearts of Americans—are not nearly as cold as the ice that Nancy Kerrigan has performed on so magically. Citing—but never explaining—"famous rule 5.05," the organization that governs figure skating in the United States awarded Nancy Kerrigan a spot on the Olympic team, even though she'd been robbed of her chance to compete in Detroit. The only caveat was that Nancy's injuries had to heal by February 6. By that time, she would have to prove she was physically ready to compete in Lillehammer. The decision had come down eight minutes after Tonya won the gold. Michelle Kwan graciously accepted, and even agreed with, the ruling.

Ever quotable Evy Scotvold seconded the rationale that had gone into the official decision: "We can't let a vicious criminal assault decide they (sic) can take someone off the Olympic team. If she heals, she has to go. Otherwise, we're honoring the attack."

In a photo that would become nearly as famous as the Nancy-in-pain shot, the full U.S. Figure Skating Olympic team posed for a group portrait. Dead center were Tonya Harding and Nancy Kerrigan. They exchanged a few words, as Nancy would later relate in a televised interview. Nancy: "Congratulations, you skated great last night." Tonya: "I hope you feel better."

The Kerrigans were persuaded to hold a small press conference before leaving Detroit. Brenda, her mind still reeling from the turn of events, said, "We can't believe that any human being would deliberately—*deliberately*—hurt her." More jaded observers, of course, *could* think of someone who might want to cripple the then-reigning U.S. Figure Skating champ. To more than a few, it seemed like "déjà vu all over again"—shades of the Texas woman who tried to put her daughter's cheerleading rival out of commission by knocking off her mom; shades of the person who stabbed Monica Seles so her rival, Steffi Graf, would take a tennis title. For some, it didn't seem too far a reach that a rival figure skater might be connected with, if not behind, the attack.

If Nancy suspected as much, she didn't let it show. Instead, she put on her bravest game face and announced, "I'll do anything I can to get myself mentally and physically ready." With that, the Kerrigan clan boarded an east-bound plane and headed home to Boston.

The same day that Nancy and her family left Detroit, police there received the first break in the case. A phone call came in from a woman who insisted on speaking with Deputy Chief Benny Napoleon, the police officer she'd seen on TV—he seemed to be in charge of the "Kerrigan case," and she had some information to share. Months earlier, she divulged, she'd heard a tape recording. On it, three men were plotting a crippling assault on Nancy Kerrigan. The caller chose to remain anonymous; she did, however, reveal the identities of the men on the tape. Authorities immediately began tracing telephone records of the trio, looking to tie them together.

With that tip, the investigative ball got rolling. It was headed westward, toward Portland, Oregon. Tonya Harding's home turf.

The second tip came to the FBI. It corroborated the first, only with much more damaging and concrete evidence. The source was Gary Crowe, a teacher at Pioneer Pacific College, a small vocational school outside of Portland. Earlier, a student named Eugene Saunders—who happened to be a born-again Christian minister—had told Mr. Crowe about a tape played for him by a fellow student in his paralegal studies class just after the Kerrigan attack. The man with the tape was Shawn Eric Eckhardt, a twenty-six-year-old, 350-pound braggart. On the tape, reported Mr. Saunders, was a conversation among three men. One was Shawn, another was an old high school buddy of Shawn's,

Jeff Gillooly. Jeff's voice was heard saying, "Why don't we just kill her?" and Shawn replied, "We don't need to kill her. Let's just hit her in the leg."

As Eugene Saunders knew, Eckhardt—who'd played the tape for him because he feared the hit men were now coming after him—was Tonya Harding's bodyguard. Jeff Gillooly was Harding's ex-husband, who still lived with the skater.

As the news became public, other witnesses soon began to show up at police headquarters. All were classmates of Shawn Eckhardt, all had similar tales to tell. Eckhardt had tried to bribe one of *them* to smash Nancy; when that bewildered student turned him down, Shawn had merely shrugged and said, "I've got a hit in Detroit. I'll just have to send my team." Later, in front of many class members, he actually said, "We got her. We got Kerrigan."

The FBI and local police in both Portland and Detroit acted swiftly to follow Shawn Eckhardt's trail: it led directly to one Derrick Smith, twenty-nine—who would turn out to have been the driver of the getaway car—and to his nephew, twenty-year-year-old weight lifter Shane Standt, the man in black who had bludgeoned Nancy Kerrigan. Day by day, more gruesome details emerged. Apparently the plot had been in the works for a while, and Shane had been stalking Nancy. He'd even flown to

Boston to try and do the deed on her home ice; it was only because he'd failed there that the hit happened in Detroit. By January 12, less than a week after the attack, the arrests of the bumbling attackers seemed imminent.

No one involved in the case believed that any of these three inept criminals could have been the brains behind the crippling plot: they suspected who *was*, but had no hard evidence to prove it. They'd heard about the tape, but had never listened to it themselves. Shawn Eckhardt had implicated Jeff, but still, that wasn't enough to go on.

The eyes of the police, the eyes of the FBI, and certainly the eyes of the media were focused squarely on Jeff Gillooly and Tonya Harding. They both strongly denied any involvement with the terrible attack on Nancy. Jeff's quote: "I have more faith in my wife than to bump off the competition." Tonya's: "If anyone wanted to beat Nancy, it was me." Then, referring to their upcoming meeting at Lillehammer, and with astounding insensitivity to Nancy's painful predicament, Tonya declared, "I'm going to whip her butt."

As the second week of January drew to a close, the authorities had their work cut out for them. So did Nancy Kerrigan.

* * *

Back on the East Coast, Nancy had retreated to Stoneham and the loving, nurturing circle of her family, friends, and physicians. "Camp Kerrigan" was officially set up, headquartered at Dan and Brenda's: it was from their front door that the world would witness—via the constant coverage of the press reps who camped outside—Nancy's rehabilitation. The young woman who had worked so hard to come back mentally and physically would just have to start all over. This time, it was the physical part of her rehab that demanded priority: she would need to prove to the USFSA and U.S. Olympic Committee that she was in top form to skate for the United States. The deadline for her examination by USOC doctors and a panel of judges was February 6—there wasn't very much time.

Nancy started by getting an MRI (magnetic resonance imaging), overseen by Dr. Steven DeFossez in Peabody, Massachusetts. The process, though not at all painful, took 110 long minutes, during which Nancy lay on her back and listened to rock music on her headphones. To her great relief, the MRI revealed no fracture or hidden damage to her kneecap or ligaments. Nancy next saw her orthopedic surgeon, Dr. Mahlon Bradley, of Salem, Massachusetts. Her first examination revealed only a thirty-seven-degree range of motion in her knee; only twenty-four hours later, however, that range had more than doubled, to seventy-five degrees. Under her doctor's supervision, Nancy embarked on a rigorous course of physical therapy, including stretching and bending exercises and aerobics, alternated with hydrotherapy workouts in the pool. Nancy dived headlong into her new regime. "It's a lot of hard work getting back. I'm pushing myself a lot harder than I thought I could have." This, after all, is a girl who knew all about focusing and was no longer afraid of hard work. That dedication served her well.

Of course, there was another battle to be waged: for Nancy's reconditioning had its emotional aspects as well. How could it not? Although she refused to adopt a victim's mentality, Nancy in fact *had* been victimized; like anyone in that position, she would need time and professional guidance. She admitted right away that the fear was still with her. "I don't know how long I'll be looking over my shoulder," she said. Once, an ordinary bag of potato chips threw her for a loop! As she explained to *People* magazine, "I was at a party, . . . watching a little kid. Suddenly, I turned around, and there was someone with a bag of potato chips . . . close to my head. It scared me for a second—and I jumped."

Nancy also admitted to TV correspondent Connie Chung that although she used to sleep pretty soundly, now even her most restful hours had been disrupted. "When this first happened, I kept waking up at night. I don't usually remember my dreams, but my whole body would just jerk and twitch and wake me up, and I'd grab my knee. It must have been some sort of nightmare."

Not surprisingly, Nancy turned to the woman who had helped her so much the year before, sports psychologist Cindy Adams, who was quoted as saying, "Nancy Kerrigan's not a victim, she's a survivor. That's how we're going to look at this. . . . She's a strong individual and she's loved a lot—and that helps a great deal." Nancy and Dr. Adams began daily sessions, and in record time, Nancy had started to feel better. In fact, Nancy and her doctors attributed her rapid recovery on both fronts to the fact that at the time of the attack, she was in the best shape of her life, mentally *and* physically.

Meanwhile, the media frenzy continued outside the tidy house in Stoneham, and Nancy's relatives came around to help—not only by supplying loving support, but also in more practical ways. Get Well mail for Nancy came in by the bushel; it would take an entire crew of relatives just to sort through it all. The letters came from all over the country— some by Federal Express; some were sent to the local paper, the *Stoneham Independent*; some were simply addressed: "Nancy Kerrigan, Massachusetts." The correspondents ranged from crayon-carrying kids to ex-Presidents. "We are so thankful you weren't harmed. We both know how difficult it can be to live in the public eye," wrote Ronald and Nancy Reagan.

No one who really knew Nancy Kerrigan ever doubted her ability to come back from this devastating blow. Her parents, of course, felt the deepest concern—yet they were the first to state that she would be just fine. "I don't believe she needs any help to get over this," Brenda had said. "She's tough. She's strong." Dan didn't disagree. "She's a fighter. She's working very hard on her leg and her skating. She's got a good head on her shoulders. She'll handle it."

When the Kerrigans weren't granting around-the-dining-room table interviews inside, they still had the legions of reporters camped outside to deal with. Graciously, Nancy tried to accommodate as many as she could. There were almost daily briefings, especially as more of the bizarre details of the case started to surface. Even as the evidence began to point more and more resolutely toward the Gillooly gang, a dignified Nancy refused to speculate. She would say only, "I'll never understand it because I can't think that viciously." Tragically for her, someone else could.

* * *

Back in Portland, police and the FBI were working overtime to crack the case wide open. They had
their sights set on Jeff Gillooly and began examin-
ing his bank records, hoping for a paper trail that
might link Jeff to the other three criminals who had
already been arrested on conspiracy to commit assault charges. It didn't take very long for the authorities to find enough. For there had been a
number of suspicious transactions—Jeff had with-
drawn a total of $9,000 in cash in late December,
and police learned that some of that money was
paid to Shawn, who in turn wired it to Derrick
Smith. Gillooly insisted the payments were simply
for bodyguard services, but as the stoolies began
spilling more information, it looked more likely
that the money had been used to pay for the attack.
What was not clear was where the money had
come from in the first place. Jeff was unemployed,
and he and Tonya had recently been evicted from
their apartment for failure to pay the rent. Tonya, of
course, received financial support from sponsors
and grants from the USFSA—had any of *that*
money been used for the attack? It was later alleged
that Tonya *did* receive $10,000 of her grant
money—a check she allegedly endorsed to Jeff.
Still, it couldn't be proved that her money was used
for illegal purposes. What the bank and phone rec-

ords *did* clearly prove was a direct connection between the now four coconspirators.

As Tonya herself continued to steadfastly claim she had neither any involvement nor prior knowledge of the assault, she was skating—as every headline seemed to blast all over the country—on increasingly thin ice. Shawn, Shane, et al., had come up with another shocker, clearly implicating Jeff, if not Tonya herself. Check the phone records, they said: In late December, there were a series of calls made to the Tony Kent Arena in Cape Cod to find out Nancy's training schedule, in hopes of crippling the skater at her home rink. The calls were traced to a cabin where Tonya and Jeff lived. Shawn, whose story has changed several times, went further, insisting that not only was Tonya in on it, but she'd been annoyed that things weren't moving fast enough. The hulking ex-bodyguard told the *Portland Oregonian* newspaper that Tonya "was pissed off and disappointed that these guys weren't able to do what they said they were gonna do. And why hasn't it happened yet?" . . . "You know, you need to stop screwing around with this and get it done."

On January 18, Tonya herself agreed to an interview with the authorities—it took ten hours to complete. At the end, the shaken skater announced she was separating (yet again) from Jeff—who would formally be arrested the following morning, charged with second degree conspiracy to commit assault—but she still believed in him and hoped her fans still believed in her. In fact, many did. For although the new evidence seemed to threaten Tonya's place on the Olympic team, a wave of support for the Portland skater began to rise up. The Tonya Harding Fan Club—an ad hoc group of admirers bound by their empathy for the beleaguered skater—vocalized their support. They showed up at her daily practices with signs and banners proclaiming her innocence and her right to go to the Olympics. That, in itself, was becoming quite the hot topic. Opinions were as diverse as they were heated.

Tonya Harding had not yet been charged with any crime—nor, at this point, had she admitted knowing anything—yet there were many who already felt she should not get a ticket to Lillehammer. This school held that guilt by association rendered her a poor choice to represent her country in the Olympics. If she went, the heat of media scrutiny would be on her—and not on the games themselves. In that case, what would the United States look like in the eyes of the world? And besides, wasn't there some kind of USFSA rule that said even if you qualified on athletic ability, if you demonstrated "unsportsmanlike" behav-

ior, or were potentially disrupting, you could be
booted? There is such a stipulation, but should it be
invoked, others warned, Tonya could probably sue
the organization; and without further evidence
against her, she'd probably win.

Other anti-Tonya arguments took the tack that
even if she did go, mightn't the judges be biased
against her? Even if she landed a "quadruple Axel,"
it was said, she wouldn't win a medal. And what
about the effect her showing up would have on
Nancy? Wouldn't it be an unnecessary distraction
for her to have Tonya as a teammate? Certainly,
Evy Scotvold thought so when he said that it would
be an unfair burden on his skater.

Sportswriter/novelist Frank Deford stated his
opinion (on a tabloid TV show) that Tonya was already perceived as such a villain, that she'd probably be booed if she showed up in Lillehammer.
"Talk about a skunk at a garden party!" he'd
hooted.

Not everyone lined up against Tonya, however.
A poll taken by *Newsweek* magazine in mid-
January showed only 18 percent of those asked
thought Tonya should not be allowed to go. Another 18 percent said she should. The vast majority
of respondents, however, took a "wait and see" attitude. Tonya could go—as long as she wasn't ac-
cused of any wrongdoing.

Opinion was mixed, strangely enough, even on Nancy's home turf, where fair-minded individuals felt that Tonya Harding should enjoy the "innocent until proven guilty" assumption on which our criminal justice system is based.

Tonya herself took part in a little damage control by appearing on ABC's *Prime Time* and sweetly saying, "I believe God is watching over me. Maybe he believes it's time for something good to happen to me." That bad things had happened to her was shown by a bit of spin doctoring that Tonya herself probably didn't even have a hand in. It was in the form of a seven-year-old documentary video tape of a teenage Tonya made by a (then) student for a college project. Aired on *60 Minutes* in mid-January, the tape revealed an awful lot about Tonya's tough times growing up—the poverty and instability of her life, and very poignantly, the rough relationship between Tonya and her mom.

Nothing, in fact, could have highlighted the differences between Tonya Harding and Nancy Kerrigan more clearly than that tape. For no matter what the public perception of Tonya had been before, watching her speak on the phone with her mother, you had to feel sorry for her. Apparently, Tonya had just done less than spectacularly her first trip to the Nationals. Judging from Tonya's tone of voice and choice of words, her mother's reaction must have been to belittle her. "What a bitch," Tonya said as she put the phone down.

Granted, Nancy was an innocent victim, and there was speculation that Tonya might have been involved in the attack. But, after watching the tape, it appeared that Nancy had the advantage of a loving, supportive family, while Tonya had none.

But the Tonya backers were balanced, if not outweighed, by the Tonya backstabbers—many from her own family. For in the crazy days that ensued, Tonya's blood relations almost never came to her defense. Viewers listened to impassioned statements made by Tonya's skating mentors: her current coach Diane Rawlinson, who said, "She's innocent. She trained hard and deserves to go," and her former coach Dody Teachman both rose to Tonya's defense. But there was very little from her mom LaVona, who once told *Sports Illustrated* that "Tonya has a vivid imagination. She has a tendency to tell tall tales." Now, LaVona was saying, albeit weakly, "All she said to me was, 'I didn't do it, Mom.' That's good enough for me." Tonya's stepdad James Golden just "hoped" it wasn't true; he didn't "think" Tonya could be involved. If her biological father commented at all, it wasn't widely reported. In fact, those relatives who were interviewed, mostly on tabloid TV, had only nasty things to say about Tonya. Anyone with an ax to grind came out swinging—including the woman motorist at whom Tonya allegedly swung a baseball bat for not turning a corner quickly enough. One relative called her "heartless"; another pointed to her "mean streak." With family like that, Tonya didn't really need enemies.

Back in Boston Nancy's recovery was proceeding rapidly. She worked daily with her physical therapists, and her routine—riding a stationary bike to strengthen her knee, swimming, doing aerobics, and even practicing her skating program on a gym floor and in the swimming pool—had produced excellent results. The swelling on her knee was "way down," she could almost extend her leg fully, and she was walking without any perceptible limp. "My leg is going to be okay," she told reporters. She managed to duck the media for her first trip back to the rink. At two A.M. on January 16, with her parents, coach, and physician at her side, Nancy laced up her skates and took her first tentative steps back onto the ice. It took great courage—what if she fell and the pain returned? What if she was trying too soon and reinjured herself? With the deadline approaching, there was no time to come back from yet another injury. There was no time to waste, either. So, summoning up her courage, she skated, at first tentatively, and then more authoritatively. Naturally, she did no jumps that first night out, but amazingly, she wanted to! "I went through my whole program [but] with no jumps or jump spins," Nancy told her hometown newspaper. "I was glad to be out there. I was stiff at first, but I loosened up more and more. . . . I need to do more stretching. It's not painful, just tight. . . . It was boring! I wanted to do more jumps."

In fact, Nancy later admitted to the paper that she actually had fallen during that first foray on the ice, while going through some normal footwork. She'd recovered quickly, though.

Nancy's emotional rehabilitation was proceeding on course as well. After awhile, she could honestly say, "When I'm on the ice, nothing really affects me. It's just something that happened. I'm working really hard to work through it."

It had to help that the residents of Stoneham— whatever their private opinions on Tonya's eligibility—had come together very publicly in support of their hometown heroine. How proud of Nancy was Stoneham? The newspaper inserted a two-page, color, "We Love You Nancy Kerrigan" poster in one issue: shopkeepers and homeowners proudly displayed it in their windows. Billboards, in a town where you really don't see very many, went up advertising support. A beautiful oil painting of Nancy in action hangs at the Stoneham Public Library. The roadway into the Stoneham Ice Arena was christened with a new sign—"Nancy Kerrigan Way."

A little more than two weeks after the attack, Nancy was able to resume her jumps—she must have been overjoyed when she realized that she really *was* okay. It didn't hurt when she took off and landed on her right knee: in the face of the brutal attack, her well-trained body had not failed her. In fact, Nancy was well enough that she could take a short break from training on January 21 to fly to Los Angeles and film a commercial for Reebok.

Publicly, her outlook was bright, and any comments she did make were solely about her recovery and readiness. Nancy remained dignified when asked about the plot: she refused to comment. In fact, the press had finally retreated from her front yard (not before one overzealous cameraperson accidentally smacked Brenda Kerrigan in the head with some equipment), and it looked as if the family's life could possibly start getting back to normal. Or whatever normal is when you're preparing to compete in the Olympics. In her only bow to "the incident," Nancy now had a bodyguard with her at all times. Typical of the family-centered Kerrigans, it was her brother Michael. Then, the case took a high-velocity twist, as yet another version of the plot was revealed to the national media.

* * *

It came from Tonya, of course: as one news-weekly so aptly put it, "The Other Skate Drops." On January 27, a shaky Tonya Harding, blond hair pulled primly back in a ponytail, dressed in her National Team skating warm-ups, faced a roomful of cameras and reporters in Portland, Oregon. She had a statement to read; she'd take no questions—although she certainly left plenty of them. Tonya stumbled over her words, and at several points seemed near tears.

She began by expressing her sorrow over the attack, and shame that "anyone close to me could be involved." Her victory at the nationals was unfulfilling, she allowed, because she didn't have Nancy to compete against. All well and good. Then, in what sounded like a last-ditch effort at absolution, Tonya pretty much buried herself. Instead of distancing herself from her ex-husband and his associates, she only pulled herself in deeper. She claimed to have "no prior knowledge of the planned assault," but admitted that she *did* find out afterward—as early as January 12—that people close to her "may have been" very much involved. This information she kept to herself, for a while. "I am responsible ... for failing to report things I learned about the assault when I returned home from Nationals." Tonya went on to say that her lawyers assured her she'd committed no crime by failing to immediately report what she knew.

"I know I have let you down," she told her audience, "but I have also let myself down." Tonya ended with a plea not to be taken off the Olympic team. "Despite my mistakes and my rough edges . . . I have done nothing to violate the standards of excellence, of sportsmanship, that are expected in an Olympic athlete."

If Tonya had so far failed to move her audience, only the most jaded would not have been touched by her final comments. "I have devoted my entire life to one objective: winning an Olympic medal for my country. This is my last chance."

Sadly, her last chance might have passed her by the second Nancy Kerrigan felt the cold, hard metal crash against her leg.

Nancy Kerrigan did not publicly reveal her reaction to Tonya's shocking admission. Instead, she kept her nose to the grindstone and her feet on the ice. Every day she got stronger, and, on deadline day, she was judged to be physically fit for Lillehammer. That was the first hurdle, and she'd crossed it with flying colors. The next, as it had always been, was the Olympics itself. How would she do? Everyone around her had the utmost confidence in her ability to at least medal, if not get the gold itself.

The real key to Nancy's own emotions and her resolve, however, may come from—like always— her mother. For when Brenda Kerrigan's fear and shock subsided, anger and deep determination took over. That became evident when she was asked by TV newswoman Connie Chung if, after the attack, she ever wished Nancy would hang up her skates. In a voice filled with passion and rage, Brenda Kerrigan said: "Oh, *no*! That's *not* what we're all about. That's not what this *family* is all about! *That's* givin' up! That's even all the more reason. . . . I'm not even a skater and that's when *I* get determined. Who in heaven's name do they think they *are* to try and get *you* out of this competition by hurting you? NO WAY!!" Spoken like a true fighter. If her daughter Nancy is a champion, Brenda's example is at least part of the reason why. When Nancy Kerrigan, looking toward Lillehammer, says, "I'm very determined. I've worked too hard to let this stop me. I think I'll be fine at Lillehammer and I believe I will do great," we believe her.

As for Tonya Harding, she too had crossed that first hurdle. Her name was not removed from the roster of figure skaters scheduled to represent the

United States at the Olympics. But that doesn't necessarily mean she will ever take to the ice in Norway. Right now, there are two separate investigations into Tonya's alleged involvement with the case. A Grand Jury has been impaneled in Portland to decide if there's enough evidence to indict her: although, even if there is, it doesn't necessarily mean she'll ever be convicted. This Grand Jury has until mid-February to announce its decision. Separately, the USFSA and the United States Olympic Committee are also scrupulously studying Tonya. Specifically, they're trying to determine if she misused any grant funds. Money given to skaters is supposed to be used only to defray training and other skating-related expenses. If they are convinced that Tonya took this money and knowingly gave it to her ex-husband to finance a hit against Nancy Kerrigan, that would be official grounds to take her off the team. Changes in the skating roster can be made until the very day the athletes draw for their skating order: in this case, February 21. Ominously, for Tonya, the USFSA has decided to send alternate Michelle Kwan to train in Norway for the Olympics. That way, if Tonya is disqualified before the skating starts, the United States would have another skater on hand.

And so, on February 12, when the Opening Ceremonies begin for the Winter Olympics, there is still a distinct possibility that Tonya Harding and Nancy Kerrigan will be standing side by side—though plans have already been made to ensure that they neither room nor train together in Norway. The image broadcast around the world would show two teammates who could not be further apart—the first may be one of the most unpopular women in the land; the other, America's sweetheart.

In anticipation of her first appearance on the ice at Lillehammer, Nancy mused, "I have a strange feeling there's going to be a big applause when I go out there." She's probably right. And why shouldn't there be? The gutsy skater from Stoneham came back not once, but twice.

CHAPTER ELEVEN

Nancy's Wish for the Future: "Just to be Happy and Healthy"

Win, place, or show at Lillehammer, Nancy Kerrigan's future is so bright, as the expression has it, she's gonna need shades. Beautiful, wholesome, brimming with youth, vitality and courage, Nancy Kerrigan is America's newest sweetheart, and she's poised to remain so for some time to come. Not so surprisingly, we're going to be seeing a whole lot more of her. She'll no doubt be beaming at us from countless magazine covers and screens both big and small. Count on it.

Her very first television special, scheduled to air on CBS on February 5, was but a forerunner of small-screen specials to come. This one, *Nancy Kerrigan & Friends*, was a tape-delayed (by one day) figure skating exhibition extraordinaire with a twofold purpose. Because Nancy had been denied the chance to skate at the Nationals in Detroit, she had not performed before a real audience in months, probably not the best way to head to Norway. "Skating in front of a crowd is markedly different from skating in practice," Evy Scotvold said in a press release announcing the TV show. "One is merely skating, the other is performing. Nancy needs to get the rust off her performing skills before going to Lillehammer."

The second reason was a bit more altruistic—net proceeds from the sale of tickets to the event went to several charities. The chief beneficiary was Campaign SightFirst. Nancy was excited about the special, which featured, among others, her close friend Paul Wylie. She apparently looked at it not only as a means to sharpen her skills, but also as a way to say thanks to her hometown fans and friends. Her official statement said it all: "I am thrilled by the overwhelming support I have received, particularly from the people in the Boston area. This will give me the chance to perform in public, and serve as a stepping stone toward my getting back in top form. It will also give me a chance to thank the people of Boston, and give us all the chance to raise money for causes that are very important to me and that go well beyond skating."

* * *

There's no question that Nancy will star in other television specials down the road: also she'll almost certainly be the subject of more than one television movie. As part of the growing trend toward "reality-based" TV movies, offers to film her inspiring real-life story began pouring into her agent's office the minute the news of the attack broke. So far, nothing has been officially sanctioned by the Kerrigan camp, but that doesn't mean TV production companies won't go ahead and film something anyway. No less than twenty scripts, it's said, are already in various stages of development. The press, in fact, has had a field day doing a little creative—albeit imaginary—casting. Supermodel Cindy Crawford and actress Brooke Shields have been proposed to play Nancy herself. (Julia Roberts was also suggested, but nobody could honestly think she would do a TV-movie.) As Tonya Harding, the media would cast superbrat Shannen Doherty, or perhaps problem-plagued former child actress Dana Plato. Eric Roberts and Jason Patric have been mentioned for Jeff Gillooly. Patty Duke would make a wonderful Brenda Kerrigan, and *Saturday Night Live*'s chunky Chris Farley is perfect for Shawn Eckhardt. Watch for it coming soon to a station near you!

Feature film offers have been made as well, but

movie producers want the real thing. Sums upward of $300,000 have already been mentioned to entice Nancy to skate onto the big screen. Will she accept such an offer? "Ask my agent," was Nancy's nonanswer when the subject was broached recently.

If a Nancy Kerrigan movie or TV movie isn't too far off, neither is a video. She has been mulling offers to star in a workout tape, as well as an instructional figure skating video. Either one would be a natural fit and a likely blockbuster.

Naturally, Nancy will continue to act as spokesperson for the various companies with which she's aligned. Her contracts with Campbell's Soup, Seiko, Reebok, et al. extend through the entire year; some will take her into 1995. There's bound to be more on her endorsement plate as well—especially if she shines at the Olympics. "She'll be very rich," agree the prognosticators. "She's a millionairess-in-the-making." Nancy's own agent, Jerry Solomon, has the hype down pat, speculating thusly: "If Nancy Kerrigan wins the gold medal in 1994, she potentially could be the biggest thing that sport has ever seen." Estimates of her future wealth run as high as $10 million—eclipsing the fortunes amassed by former American figure skating sweethearts Dorothy Hamill and Peggy Fleming. Is there any doubt that Nancy will use some of that money to help her family and the causes in which she believes?

Nor is Nancy about to hang up her skates after the Olympics. She has already signed on to be part of an upcoming fifty-nine-city figure skating ice show, run by promoter Tom Collins. The tour, which also figures to feature Oksana Baiul, Surya Bonaly, and Scott Davis, among other greats, will rung from April 11 to July 12: a nice chunk of the year, and a nice chunk of cash for the performers. Olympians can make between $5,000 and $15,000 per performance.

Nancy will also continue to raise cash for charity, especially for the cause closest to her heart— Campaign SightFirst. No matter what else the year—and those following—bring, Nancy Kerrigan can be counted on to hit the fund-raising trail to help others. It's a big part of what she's all about.

Indeed, Hollywood may be calling, and so may a hundred brokers, but Nancy's heart remains where it always has: close to home and hearth. Her own goals for the future are not nearly so glitzy as those others would have for her. She has said, in fact, that what she really wants to do is open a skating school to help other young hopefuls avoid some of the mistakes she made. Nancy took business courses at college with one practical eye looking forward to such a venture. They'll come in handy if she ever does open a Nancy Kerrigan Figure Skating School, or a chain of them. "Someday, I would like to teach," Nancy has acknowledged, "but only part time." Why? "I want to have a family." With her own parents, Brenda and Dan Kerrigan, as role models, it's not hard to understand why that would be one of her major goals. What else is on Nancy's personal wish list for the future? "Just to be happy and healthy," said the woman who's already wealthy in all the things that money *can't* buy, and wise enough to know it.

Indeed, no matter what the future brings, Nancy Kerrigan will always be able to count on the unconditional love and support of her family, friends, and ultimately, of millions of people who will never meet her in person, but who have already been touched and inspired by her story, and by her courage.

CHAPTER TWELVE

Kerrigan Clips:
Facts at Your Fingertips

FULL NAME: Nancy Ann Kerrigan

BIRTHDAY: October 13, 1969

BIRTHPLACE: Woburn, Massachusetts

GREW UP IN: Stoneham, Massachusetts

HEIGHT: 5′ 4″

WEIGHT: 111 lbs.

HAIR: Brown

EYES: Blue

LIVES: In a condominium in Plymouth, Massachusetts, on Cape Cod's north coast. When she's training, however, she shares a house in Sagamore Beach—also on the Cape—with other Scotvold students.

FAVORITES
  Sports: Rollerblading, bike riding, hockey, golf, skiing, snowmobiling—and figure skating!
  Music: Rock 'n' roll
  TV: Daytime soaps
  Food: Campbell's chicken noodle soup, pizza
  Clothing: On the ice it's as bright and glittery as can be; off the ice, it's the complete opposite. Nancy's into comfort over chic—jeans, sweatpants, baseball caps, and sweatshirts with logos from Emmanuel College and USA Olympics.

SHE OFTEN HANGS OUT WITH: Her brothers. They still play street hockey!

SHE COLLECTS: Baseball caps, stuffed animals

BEAUTY TIP: "Short skirts make you look taller."

SO HOW'S HER LOVE LIFE? Since the breakup with Bill Chase, she's quite single. She scoffs at rumors linking her with Michael Collins, the son of ice show promoter Tom Collins. She and Michael are only friends, she says.

WHAT SHE DOES WITH ALL HER MEDALS: "I put them away, because they tarnish so easily unless you polish them every day."

HER MOTTO: "Always dream."

ADDRESS: Fan mail should be addressed as follows: Nancy Kerrigan, c/o ProServ, 1101 Wilson Blvd., Suite 1800, Arlington, VA 22209.

More Facts
about Nancy Kerrigan
and the World
of Figure Skating

NANCY KERRIGAN

COMPETITIVE HISTORY

1994 National Senior	(Withdrew due to injury)	
1993 AT&T Pro-Am Challenge		1st
1993 Piruetten		1st
1993 Hershey's Kisses Pro-Am Championships		2nd
1993 World Championships		5th
1993 National Senior		1st
1992 Chrysler Concorde Pro-Am Challenge		1st
1992 Skate America		2nd
1992 World Championships		2nd
1992 Olympic Winter Games		3rd
1992 National Senior		2nd
1991 Nations Cup		1st
1991 Trophee Lalique		3rd
1991 World Championships		3rd
1991 National Senior		3rd
1991 Eastern Senior		1st
1990 Trophee Lalique		3rd
1990 Goodwill Games		5th
1990 U.S. Olympic Festival		1st
1990 Skate Electric		3rd
1990 National Senior		4th
1990 Eastern Senior		1st
1989 Skate America		5th
1989 U.S. Olympic Festival		3rd

1989	World University Games	3rd
1989	National Senior	5th
1989	Eastern Senior	1st
1989	New England Senior	1st
1988	Novarat Trophy	1st
1988	Karl Schafer Memorial	1st
1988	National Collegiate	1st
1988	National Collegiate	3rd(flg)
1988	National Senior	12th
1988	New England Senior	1st
1987	NHK Trophy	5th
1987	U.S. Olympic Festival	2nd(Team)
1987	National Junior	4th
1987	Eastern Junior	2nd
1987	New England Junior	3rd

What You Need to Know to Watch Nancy Kerrigan Skate at the Olympics

The key requirements for athletes at the highest level of women's figure skating are form, style, concentration, technique, and the ability to excel under pressure. Each competition is made up of two distinct parts—the *technical*, or short, program and the *free skating*, or long, program.

The technical program is performed first, and determines 33.3 percent of each skater's total score. The sport's governing body has chosen eight required elements (three spins, three jumps, and two footwork moves) that must be included in the technical programs by each woman at the 1994 Lillehammer Olympics.

The eight moves are:

1) Double Axel
2) Double Jump
3) Two Double Jumps or a Double and a Triple Jump (with no step in between)
4) Flying Spin
5) Layback or Sideways Leaning Spin
6) Spin Combination with Only One Foot Change and At Least Two Position Changes
7) Spiral Step Sequence
8) Non-spiral Step Sequence

These eight moves must be completed within a two-minute, forty-second time limit. They can be performed in any order to the accompaniment of music of the skater's choosing. The judges will then award two different scores that rate *technical merit* (how skillfully the moves were executed) and *artistic impression.*

In the four-minute-long free skating program, which counts for 66.7 percent of the skater's total score, there are no required moves or jumps. Each woman selects her own music and choreographs a routine of footwork, artistic moves, jumps, and spins that will serve to showcase her fundamentals and her artistry for the judges. As with the short program, two scores are presented; here, the judges take into account the difficulty level of the routine, as well as the skill level of the performance and the overall artistic impression.

In each category, the judges deduct points for mistakes and omissions, and rank each skater on a six-point scale as follows:

0	not skated
1	bad, very poor
2	poor
3	average
4	good
5	excellent
6	perfect

Decimals (4.9, 5.6, 6.0) are used to be more precise in scoring.

Olympic Women's Figure Skating Medalists

	GOLD	SILVER	BRONZE
1908 London, GBR	Madge Syers, GBR	Elsa Rendschmidt, GER	Dorothy Greenhough, GBR
1920 Antwerp, BEL	Magda Julin–Mauroy, SWE	Svea Noren, SWE	Theresa Weld, USA
1924 Chamonix, FRA	Herma Plank–Szabo, AUT	Beatrix Loughran, USA	Ethel Muckett, GBR
1928 St. Moritz, SUI	Sonja Henie, NOR	Fritzi Burger, AUT	Beatrix Loughran, USA
1932 Lake Placid, USA	Sonja Henie, NOR	Fritzi Burger, AUT	Maribel Vinson, USA
1936 Garmisch Partenkirchen, GER	Sonja Henie, NOR	Cecilia Colledge, GBR	Vivi–Anne Hulten, SWE
1940 No Games held			
1944 No Games held			
1948 St. Moritz, SUI	Barbara Ann Scott, CAN	Eva Pawlik, AUT	Jeannette Altwegg, GBR
1952 Oslo, NOR	Jeannette Altwegg, GBR	Tenley Albright, USA	Jacqueline du Bief, FRA
1956 Cortina, ITA	Tenley Albright, USA	Carol Heiss, USA	Ingrid Wendl, AUT
1960 Squaw Valley, USA	Carol Heiss, USA	Sjoukje Dijkstra, HOL	Barbara Roles, USA
1964 Innsbruck, AUT	Sjoukje Dijkstra, HOL	Regine Heitzer, AUT	Petra Burka, CAN
1968 Grenoble, FRA	Peggy Fleming, USA	Gabriele Seyfert, GDR	Hana Maskova, CZE
1972 Sapporo, FRA	Beatrix Schuba, AUT	Karen Magnussen, CAN	Janet Lynn, USA
1976 Innsbruck, AUT	Dorothy Hamill, USA	Dianne du Leeuw, HOL	Christine Errath, GDR
1980 Lake Placid, USA	Anett Poetzsch, GDR	Linda Fratianne, USA	Dagmar Lurz, FRG
1984 Sarajevo, YUG	Katarina Witt, GDR	Rosalynn Summers, USA	Kira Ivanova, URS
1988 Calgary, CAN	Katarina Witt, GDR	Elizabeth Manley, CAN	Debi Thomas, USA
1992 Albertville, FRA	Kristi Yamaguchi, USA	Midori Ito, JPN	Nancy Kerrigan, USA

World
Women's Figure Skating Champions

1906 Madge Syers, GBR
1907 Madge Syers, GBR
1908 Lily Kronberger, HUN
1909 Lily Kronberger, HUN
1910 Lily Kronberger, HUN
1911 Lily Kronberger, HUN
1912 Oprika von Horvath, HUN
1913 Oprika von Horvath, HUN
1914 Oprika von Horvath, HUN
1915 No championship held
1916 No championship held
1917 No championship held
1918 No championship held
1919 No championship held

1920 No championship held
1921 No championship held
1922 Herma Plank-Szabo, AUT
1923 Herma Plank-Szabo, AUT
1924 Herma Plank-Szabo, AUT
1925 Herma Plank-Szabo, AUT
1926 Herma Plank-Szabo, AUT
1927 Sonja Henie, NOR
1928 Sonja Henie, NOR
1929 Sonja Henie, NOR
1930 Sonja Henie, NOR
1931 Sonja Henie, NOR
1932 Sonja Henie, NOR
1933 Sonja Henie, NOR
1934 Sonja Henie, NOR
1935 Sonja Henie, NOR
1936 Sonja Henie, NOR
1937 Cecilia Colledge, GBR
1938 Megan Taylor, GBR
1939 Megan Taylor, GBR
1940 No championship held
1941 No championship held
1942 No championship held
1943 No championship held
1944 No championship held
1945 No championship held
1946 No championship held
1947 Barbara Ann Scott, CAN

1948 Barbara Ann Scott, CAN

1949 Alena Vrzanova, CZE

1950 Alena Vrzanova, CZE

1951 Jeannette Altwegg, GBR

1952 Jacqueline du Bief, FRA

1953 Tenley Albright, USA

1954 Gundi Busch, FRG

1955 Tenley Albright, USA

1956 Carol Heiss, USA

1957 Carol Heiss, USA

1958 Carol Heiss, USA

1959 Carol Heiss, USA

1960 Carol Heiss, USA

1961 No championship held

1962 Sjoukje Dijkstra, HOL

1963 Sjoukje Dijkstra, HOL

1964 Sjoukje Dijkstra, HOL

1965 Petra Burka, CAN

1966 Peggy Fleming, USA

1967 Peggy Fleming, USA

1968 Peggy Fleming, USA

1969 Gabriele Seyfert, GDR

1970 Gabriele Seyfert, GDR

1971 Beatrix Schurba, AUT

1972 Beatrix Schurba, AUT

1973 Karen Magnussen, CAN

1974 Christine Errath, GDR

1975 Dianne de Leeuw, HOL

1976 Dorothy Hamill, USA
1977 Linda Fratianne, USA
1978 Anett Poetzsch, GDR
1979 Linda Fratianne, USA
1980 Anett Poetzsch, GDR
1981 Denise Beillmann, SUI
1982 Elaine Zayak, USA
1983 Rosalynn Sumners, USA
1984 Katarina Witt, GDR
1985 Katarina Witt, GDR
1986 Debi Thomas, USA
1987 Katarina Witt, GDR
1988 Katarina Witt, GDR
1989 Midori Ito, JPN
1990 Jill Trenary, USA
1991 Kristi Yamaguchi, USA
1992 Kristi Yamaguchi, USA
1993 Oksana Baiul, UKR

U.S. Women's
Figure Skating
Champions

1914 Theresa Weld
1915 No championship held
1916 No championship held
1917 No championship held
1918 Rosemary Beresford
1919 No championship held
1920 Theresa Weld
1921 Theresa Blanchard
1922 Theresa Blanchard
1923 Theresa Blanchard
1924 Theresa Blanchard
1925 Beatrix Loughran
1926 Beatrix Loughran
1927 Beatrix Loughran

1928 Maribel Vinson
1929 Maribel Vinson
1930 Maribel Vinson
1931 Maribel Vinson
1932 Maribel Vinson
1933 Maribel Vinson
1934 Suzanne Davis
1935 Maribel Vinson
1936 Maribel Vinson
1937 Maribel Vinson
1938 Joan Tozzer
1939 Joan Tozzer
1940 Joan Tozzer
1941 Jane Vaughn
1942 Jane Vaughn
1943 Gretchen Merrill
1944 Gretchen Merrill
1945 Gretchen Merrill
1946 Gretchen Merrill
1947 Gretchen Merrill
1948 Gretchen Merrill
1949 Yvonne Sherman
1950 Yvonne Sherman
1951 Sonya Klopfer
1952 Tenley Albright
1953 Tenley Albright
1954 Tenley Albright
1955 Tenley Albright

1956 Tenley Albright
1957 Carol Heiss
1958 Carol Heiss
1959 Carol Heiss
1960 Carol Heiss
1961 Laurence Owen
1962 Barbara Roles
1963 Lorraine Hanlon
1964 Peggy Fleming
1965 Peggy Fleming
1966 Peggy Fleming
1967 Peggy Fleming
1968 Peggy Fleming
1969 Janet Lynn
1970 Janet Lynn
1971 Janet Lynn
1972 Janet Lynn
1973 Janet Lynn
1974 Dorothy Hamill
1975 Dorothy Hamill
1976 Dorothy Hamill
1977 Linda Fratianne
1978 Linda Fratianne
1979 Linda Fratianne
1980 Linda Fratianne
1981 Elaine Zayak
1982 Rosalynn Sumners
1983 Rosalynn Sumners

1984 Rosalynn Sumners
1985 Tiffany Chin
1986 Debi Thomas
1987 Jill Trenary
1988 Debi Thomas
1989 Jill Trenary
1990 Jill Trenary
1991 Tonya Harding
1992 Kristi Yamaguchi
1993 Nancy Kerrigan
1994 Tonya Harding

Glossary of Skating Terms

Accountant: A skating official who compiles and computes the judges' scores to determine the final ranking of skaters at a competition.

Axel Jump: A highly difficult jump in which a skater takes off from the forward outside edge of a skate and lands on the back outside edge of the opposite foot. Skaters perform single (1½ revolutions), double (2½ revolutions), and triple (3½ revolutions) Axels. The Axel is the only jump that begins while skating forward.

Crossovers: A technique for gathering speed and turning corners (either backward or forward) by crossing one foot over the other.

Edges: The sides (inside and outside) of a skate blade. Each side is also divided into forward and backward edges, making a total of four.

Flip Jump: A toe pick–assisted jump, in which a skater takes off from one back inside edge and lands on the opposite foot's back outside edge.

Jump Combination: A sequence of two or more jumps in which the landing edge of one is the take-off edge of the next, so that there are no steps in between.

Layback Spin: An upright spin characterized by dropped-back head and shoulders and an arched back.

Loop Jump: An edge jump in which a skater takes off from and lands on the same back outside edge.

Lutz Jump: A complex toe pick–assisted jump in which a skater takes off from a back outside edge and lands on the opposite foot's back outside edge. To perform this jump, a skater makes a wide, curved approach, taps the ice with her toe pick, and rotates in the air back against the curve.

Referee: The skating official who serves as chairman of the panel of judges and has full authority over all aspects of an event.

Salchow: An edge jump marked by a take-off from a back inside edge and a landing on the opposite foot's back outside edge.

Sit Spin: A spin in which the skater's body is near the ice with the skating leg bent at the knee and the free (nonskating) leg fully extended.

Toe Loop: A toe pick–assisted jump in which a skater takes off from a back outside edge and lands on the same edge.

Toe Picks: The teeth that are situated at the very front of the skate blade that help skaters perform jumps and spins.

About the Author

RANDI REISFELD is the bestselling author of over a dozen books about young celebrities. As editorial director of *16* magazine, she has interviewed and written about the most popular stars of television, movies, and rock 'n' roll. Her most recent books for young adults are *Joey Lawrence*; *Melrose Place: Meet the Stars of the Hottest TV Show*; *The Stars of Beverly Hills 90210: Their Lives and Loves*; *Lovin' Luke: The Luke Perry Story*; *Marky Mark and the Funky Bunch*; and *The Official Baywatch Fact File*. In addition, she has written the definitive how-to guide for young people who want to break into show business: *So You Want to Be a Star! A Teenager's Guide to Breaking into Show Business*.

Venturing out of the celebrity scene for the adult market, she has written *The Bar/Bat Mitzvah Survival Guide*, and coauthored *When No Means No: A Guide to Sexual Harassment*.

Ms. Reisfeld's work has also appeared in *The New York Times*, *First For Women*, *Scholastic*, and *Women's World Magazine*. Her articles are syndicated throughout Great Britain and Europe; she writes a regular celebrity gossip column for *Star* magazine in Australia.

She lives in the New York area with her husband and teenage children—and is a big, if recent, fan of figure skating.